Backpacking's Triple Crown: the Junior Version

Hiking the Best of America's Long Trails

By Jim Rahtz

Contents

There's been an explosion of interest in thru-hiking recently. Books and movies have given the public a taste of the rewards and challenges of long distance hiking. While neither Cheryl Strayed (Wild) or Bill Bryson (A Walk in the Woods) completed a thru-hike of the trails they were hiking, the tales of their journeys were epic enough to unleash a flood of interest in the better known long trails of the U.S.

Despite their growing popularity, it is still a very select group that has completed a thru-hike of the Appalachian Trail, Pacific Crest Trail or the Continental Divide Trail. The commitment required is immense. To cover the more than 2,000 miles each trail traverses, he or she gives up the comforts of home, family and friends for five months or more. They also give up their job and even the potential of a job for that same period.

Those that have hiked all three of the trails are members of an even more exclusive club. The few that have completed this "Triple Crown" of hiking have covered nearly 8,000 miles and have a total hiking time of around a year and a half. This level of dedication to hiking is not possible for most. It is however, feasible to experience the best of these trails and still have a life. That's right, it is possible to be a thru-hiker without major disruption to your career or family. It's even possible to hike the Triple Crown; just the Junior Version.

The Junior Version of hiking's Triple Crown? You might be saying to yourself, "Where did he come up with that?"

In 2014 I was attempting a thru-hike of the 486 mile Colorado Trail. I had enjoyed shorter backpacking trips, loved the scenery of the Rockies and felt my life needed a new challenge. It was one of those "bucket list" kind of things. The hike itself turned into a great experience that I was glad to have undertaken. The trail experience was everything that I had hoped as I walked through an incredible mountain environment on a path that was often shared by both the Colorado Trail and the Continental Divide Trail.

It was near the finish after a tough 22-mile day that I found myself sharing a campfire with several other thru-hikers. Gimpy, a guy in his 60s who had a long history of hiking, was talking about his other thru-hikes. At one point he asked me about hiking the Appalachian Trail (AT). I replied that I didn't have the time or a strong desire to hike the whole AT. I was however, thinking about hiking shorter "long trails" such as the John Muir Trail (JMT) through the Sierra Mountains of California. He suggested that after the JMT I should hike the Long Trail in Vermont. That way I would have hiked some of the best of the three foremost cross-country trails.

Not a bad thought. That's when a plan was born for a new challenge. I could do the Triple Crown of Hiking, only the Junior Version! The Colorado Trail is considered by many to be the best part of the Continental Divide Trail. The John Muir Trail is an iconic hike that shares much of its length with the Pacific Crest Trail. And the Long Trail, which runs through Vermont and shares 100 miles with the AT, crosses the very spot that inspired the AT. Thru-hiking this Triple Crown would not only be epic, but achievable.

So just what constitutes a thru-hike? That definition seems to change depending upon who you talk to. At the end of <u>A Walk in the Woods,</u> despite walking less than half its length, Katz declared, "I hiked the Appalachian Trail. I hiked it in snow and I hiked it in heat. I hiked it in the South and I hiked it in the North. I hiked it till my feet bled. I hiked the Appalachian Trail."

At the other extreme, there are purists that feel that unless you walk every single inch of a trail with no allowance for alternate routes, slackpacking or other assistance, you haven't "really" thru-hiked. That's why a hiker often uses the refrain, "Hike your own hike." It is an easy response to someone wanting to impose their idea of what constitutes a thru-hike onto you.

My idea of a thru-hike? I relate thru-hiking to another long term and potentially life changing experience; getting a college degree. Now, no one questions whether you attended every class or correctly answered every question on every test before deciding whether or not you "really" earned your degree. That would be ridiculous. A degree is given for successfully completing the broader requirements/experience of the program.

My requirements for completing a thru-hike are comparable. The hike has to be completed in one season (a fairly universal requirement). The hike must include the beginning, end, major highlights and the vast majority of the trail mileage. Keeping with the educational comparison, when I went to school, a 95 earned an A+ (highest grade). So my personal requirement for a completed thru-hike is to hike at least 95% of the trail's mileage. Additionally, most degree programs have options and I feel that alternate trails that are widely used count as acceptable substitutes. For example, on the Long Trail, there's a well-traveled blue blazed trail to the popular resupply stop, Inn on the Long Trail. That alternative trail, which was the original route of the Long Trail, may actually be used by more hikers than the official route. I walked that alternate without apology.

And so, if I could cover at least 95% of the mileage of a trail as well as round out the trail "experience" by being there for beginning, end and the highlights, then I'd confidently call myself a thru-hiker of that trail. If you disagree, feel free to "hike your own hike."

Having completed my Triple Crown Junior challenge, my hope for this book is to let others know that the challenge and accomplishment of a thru-hike is not just for those that can dedicate months at a time to the endeavor. Perhaps, after reading this, you too will consider placing one or all three of these hikes on your bucket list. Each trail is different with different challenges and different rewards. They are each significant adventures in their own right. But each can be done, either as a thru-hike or section hike, in a reasonable period of time while not overly sacrificing relationships or careers.

(If you have the paperback version of this book and are interested in seeing full color versions of the pictures, they're posted at oldmanoutdoors.net)

The Colorado Trail

Replacing the Continental Divide Trail in the Junior Triple Crown is the Colorado Trail. Dubbed "the most beautiful long trail in the world," the 486 mile long Colorado Trail (CT) is the longest and time consuming of this Triple Crown. It is also the least busy of the three trails with under 200 recognized thru-hikers completing the trail in 2014. Initial construction was completed in 1987, making it by far the newest trail as well. Beyond self-issued permits at some of the wilderness areas, no paperwork is required to hike the CT.

Winding from just south of Denver, Colorado southwest to Durango, the CT is mostly single track with significant mileage on Forest Service roads. There is one (6 mile) section of road walking. The trail winds through eight mountain ranges, six wilderness areas and some of the most beautiful scenery in the Rocky Mountains. The CT shares approximately 235 Miles with the Continental Divide Trail.

The trail itself is very well constructed and appears to be well maintained. A tent is a necessity as support structures such as shelters are noticeably absent. In my mind a hammock is not really an option due to the trail spending extended stretches above tree line.

Altitude is a significant consideration on the trail. The average elevation is over 10,000 feet and snow can remain well into the summer months. Most thru-hikers hike from the Denver southwest towards Durango. With this approach it takes a bit longer to get to the highest elevations, allowing for more time to acclimate. Specifically, the trail takes over 110 miles to reach 12,000 feet the first time. Hiking the other direction brings you to that same elevation in a steep 23 miles. Heading west from Denver also gives the parts of the trail that typically hold more snow a bit more time to melt before your arrival. That is the direction I took.

Resupply options on the trail are relatively few, but are spaced out pretty well. My stops included:

Town	Trail Mileage	Comments
Frisco	104	A free bus service has a stop right by the trail in two spots. This allows easy access to resupply and an opportunity for a 13 mile slack pack. The bus also serves Breckenridge.
Twin Lakes	175	The Twin Lakes General Store is a mile off the trail. They hold packages, have some groceries and lodging is possible nearby.
Salida	252	A hostel, several hotels, groceries and outfitter are in town. I sent a package to the Post Office. The town is 13 miles from the trail, but US 50 is a busy road and a relatively easy hitch. Also, taxi service will bring you to town for $30 (2014).

Lake City	357	A hostel, multiple hotels, groceries and outfitter are in town. I sent a package to the Post Office. The town is 17 miles from the trail but a straightforward hitch. Trail angels may also provide rides.
Silverton	411	A hostel, multiple hotels, groceries and outfitter are in town. The town is 6 miles from the trail. Options to town are a hitch, hostel arranged rides or a train. I highly recommend the train.

There are other options, but these appeared to be the best locations for my schedule and hiking speed.

In a Nutshell

Distance	**486 Miles**
Miles shared	**235 With CDT**
Days on trail	**32**
Permits required	**None in advance/Self issued**
Highlights	**Mountain scenery, wildlife, weather**
Challenges	**Distance between resupplies, elevation, remoteness**
Shelters	**Bring a tent**

A taste of the trail: One way to get a good taste of the trail is to hike the Collegiate Loop. The recently completed Collegiate West route option can be combined with the original CT to form a 160 mile loop. Resupply options of Salida and Twin Lakes are close to equidistance apart allowing for a very scenic hike with minimal logistical issues.

Another option in the Silverton-Durango area is to utilize the train as a shuttle. A few miles between one of the train stations and the trail must be navigated in some manner, but the 80 miles of trail between the towns is gorgeous.

The John Muir Trail

This trail should be on every hiker's bucket list. It is 220 miles of spectacular. The JMT shares 170 miles with the Pacific Crest Trail and by all accounts is the most scenic section of the PCT. Running from Yosemite National Park to Kings Canyon National Park, the trail travels through the Sierra Nevada Mountains to the top of Mt Whitney, the highest peak in the continental United States. Known for their beauty, the Sierras were called "The Range of Light" by John Muir.

Due to its popularity and location in National Parks the JMT is the most regulated of the major long hiking trails. Permits to hike the trail are limited and difficult to get in prime season. Per the National Park Service, only 3% of permit applications are approved. To improve the chances of getting a permit, look at the shoulder seasons rather than midsummer.

However, early season hiking may result in serious snowpack issues, especially on El Nino years. Hiking into late September can be a bit riskier as well. The bugs are gone, but wildfires are more likely, plus there's a chance of an early snow while you're out.

Another option to possibly help secure a permit is to look at alternative starting points. Most hikers try to begin at Happy Isles in Yosemite and hike south to Whitney. This approach means that the early miles are at a lower elevation and more resupply options are available as you work toward the harder conditions later in the hike. For those willing and able to start their hike straight up Mt Whitney with heavy food loads, you can also attempt to secure a Whitney Portal permit. For the non-purist, there are other possibilities.

Resupplies are interesting on the JMT. Walking north to south allows a hiker to carry much less food starting out; keeping the food weight and volume down during the first 100 miles or so. This can be important as all food legally needs to be in a bear canister for much of the trail and good sense states it should be in the canister for the entire hike.

For those starting at the Happy Isles Trailhead, a resupply can be had as quickly as Tuolumne Meadows, 20+ miles in. There is a post office there that will hold a package. Red's Meadow Resort is right off the trail at mile 61. They will hold packages for a fee and also have a small grocery store. The restaurant has some great food. During the summer, bus service to the city of Mammoth is available there.

The only resupply I used on my hike was at Vermillion Valley Resort (VVR). Stopping here involves either an 8 mile hike off the JMT or a boat ride across Lake Edison. Take the boat. This is an interesting place that's "off the grid." The whole resort is powered by a diesel generator that shuts off about 10 pm each night. However, they hold packages for a fee, have a great restaurant, a small grocery and a clean, comfortable motel. The resort is about 90 miles deep into the trail.

As this was to be my only resupply, it was a bit of a battle to cram enough food (seven days) into the bear canister to tide me over the remaining 130 miles of the trail. I did carry some additional food which I ate during my first day past the resort.

Many hikers resupply at Muir Trail Ranch (MTR) near mile 110. Packages can be sent there, but there is no available grocery to stock up on your own. This spot is very close to the halfway point of the JMT. (I realize that the trail ends at the top of Mt Whitney, mile 210, but you still have to get off the mountain which involves another 10 miles of walking.) The reason I did not stop there is because their overnight accommodations are expensive; and were booked solid. Since I was stopping at VVR, it didn't seem worth the time or cost of another resupply only 20 miles further down the trail. In addition, MTR closes for the season in Mid-September and I would have been flirting with their last day of business with no allowance for a delay during my hike.

Once past MTR, resupplies get difficult, and/or expensive. There is nothing near the trail and the cost to bring packages to the trail via pack mule made me decide to be my own pack mule and carry food for the whole stretch.

There are no blazes on the trail whatsoever, but most intersections are signed. Navigation is not difficult. On the trail I carried the JMT Pocket Atlas by Blackwoods Press. In addition, I had downloaded the Guthook JMT Trail App onto my iPhone. Both worked well at pinpointing water, campsites and the like.

If you like strikingly beautiful scenery, wildlife encounters, crystal clear lakes and streams, blue skies, high passes, summiting the continental United States' highest peak and the thought of over 100 miles of trail without a single road crossing, this is the trail for you. You're also not alone.

In a Nutshell

Distance	220 Miles
Miles shared	170 With PCT
Days on trail	13
Permits required	Yes
Highlights	Incredible mountain scenery, wildlife, weather

Challenges	Distance between resupplies, elevation, remoteness, getting permits, bear precautions
Shelters	Bring a tent

A taste of the trail: Red's Meadow to Tuolumne or Happy Isles is a 40-60 mile option that is scenic, avoids the tougher climbs and can work with available bus service.

The Long Trail

With construction starting in 1910, Vermont's "footpath in the wilderness" was the first long distance hiking trail in the United States. It runs from the Massachusetts state line north for 273 miles along the spine of the Green Mountains to within yards of the Canadian border. The Long Trail (LT) shares 104 miles with the Appalachian Trail. In addition, Stratton Mountain, on the trail, was the spot where Benton McKaye conceived of the AT.

Shelters are numerous along the trail, averaging 5 miles apart. In addition, each shelter, or four sided lodge, is placed near a water source and a latrine. Where the two trails share a path, the shelters can be crowded, especially during early August. At this time, you are likely to meet not only other LT hikers, but also both north and southbound AT thru-hikers. For a backup, it's a good idea to bring along a tent or hammock. A hammock may be the better choice as there's sometimes a shortage of flat ground, but trees are nearly always available. There's a noticeable reduction in fellow hikers north of the split.

In the south, where the LT shares a path with the AT, hiking is very reminiscent of other sections of the AT I have been on; challenging at times, yet somehow relaxing. Once the AT splits off towards the White Mountains in east, the LT rises to a whole new level of challenge. It may have been the weather, but farther north is where the famous "Vermud" began to grace my hike. There were also rock scrambles, ladders to climb, spots where I wished there were ladders to climb, slick rock slopes to slide on and several spots where my thoughts were, "You've got to be kidding me." It was on the Long Trail that, for me, backpacking became an adrenaline sport.

The AT has been described as walking through a green tunnel. While there is much of that, the LT trail designers made a point of crossing the peaks of most of the mountains. Nearly every day had at least one expansive view of the beautiful Vermont countryside. Like much of the AT, resupply options are plentiful. It is rare to hike more than 25 miles without an opportunity to reach a nearby town.

In a Nutshell

Distance	273 Miles
Miles shared	104 With AT
Days on trail	20
Permits required	No
Highlights	Other hikers, scenery, plentiful latrines (I'm a simple man)

Challenges	Trail conditions, elevation changes, weather
Shelters	Plentiful on the trail, but can be crowded. A back-up tent or hammock highly recommended

Taste of the Trail: Southern Terminus to Waterbury. Admittedly a big taste, this 180 mile hike involves all the mileage that the LT shares with the AT and a significant portion of the more difficult northern section. The hike finishes with the tough climb and descent of Vermont's highest undeveloped peak, Camels Hump. Once off Camels Hump, it is a short hitch to the town of Waterbury. There are hotels in town along with an Amtrak station. Between the train and Greyhound, it is possible to return to the starting point near Williamstown, MA

Obviously my thought was to hike all three, but if you only have the time or inclination to hike just one, you have a tough decision to make. Any one hike can be a tremendous, life changing adventure, but each is a different experience. Your individual priorities can guide you though.

Scenery and Wildlife

Each trail contains jaw dropping views worthy of a coffee table book and each is beautiful in its own way.

The Long Trail is classic eastern mountains. Much of the time is spent meandering through beech and maple trees. Because the trail runs the very spine of the Green Mountains, there are a surprising number of big views. Besides the bare peaks of Camels Hump and Mt Mansfield, several other mountains crossed are ski resorts in the winter. The cleared slopes reveal more scenery than typically found on other eastern mountains. Quite often the views also include a beautiful small town nestled down in a valley.

Clear streams abound. An occasional rock wall delineates old farm fields that have since returned to their natural state. Even the variety of shelters along the trail add visual interest to the day.

I personally did not see much wildlife. Beyond squirrels, rabbits and the occasional startling explosion of a grouse, my hike was surprisingly lacking in animal encounters. However, the area holds both deer and moose. I also saw some damage from porcupines and even bear; so they are there as well.

The Colorado Trail is quintessential big mountain hiking. Rather than follow one chain of mountains, the CT crosses eight named mountain ranges, each with its own look. The hike varies between open coniferous forests, aspen groves, high mesas and rugged alpine passes with views of mountaintops that seem to extend forever. In some drier areas, there are even cacti. While the trail averages over 10,000 feet in elevation, the object of the trail is not to climb the peaks, but travel around them. Mountaintop views are possible through side trips, but not on the CT itself.

Wildlife is prevalent on the trail and I saw quite a bit ranging from hummingbirds, chipmunks and pika up to big mammals including deer, moose, bighorn sheep and elk. Turkey and rabbit made regular appearances. Marmots were very numerous at higher elevations. There are also black bear near the trail, though I did not see any.

The John Muir Trail is strikingly beautiful for nearly all of its 220 miles. (I know it's 210, but you still have to get off Mt Whitney.) Heading south through Yosemite National Park, there is one iconic scene after another. There are many spots where multiple postcard quality views can be seen by simply turning your head. Despite being the shortest trail, it contained the most awe-inspiring beauty.

Beyond jaw dropping views of places like Half Dome, Cathedral Peak, Evolution Valley and the high passes, the JMT is about water. There are beautiful alpine lakes and countless clear streams. Even with hiking during a drought, enough melting snow was left to fill the spectacular rapids and waterfalls that travel down the mountains' steep slopes. Much of the trail appeared very dry, but water was never an issue. There is only one mountaintop view, but it's a doozy. At 14,505 feet, the summit of Mt Whitney is not only the official endpoint of the JMT, it is the highest spot in the continental United States. On a clear day, the view goes on seemingly forever.

Potential wildlife sightings on the trail are second to none as well. A good portion of the hike is within National Parks after all. All the wildlife normally thought of in a mountain wilderness lives near the JMT. Deer were thick through the lower elevations and seemingly oblivious to hikers. What really stood out during my hike was the close encounters with predators. I happened upon coyote and even a bobcat while on the trip. Multiple sightings of bear left no doubt why food canisters are required.

Logistics and Planning

There is more to hiking a long trail than just taking a long walk. First, you and your equipment have to get to the start of the trail. Finding a spot to stay each night is a daily chore. Arrangements must be made to acquire more food during the hike. Once completed, it's a real plus to be able to get back to the starting point and/or home. Each trail has some issues with logistics, but none are insurmountable.

The Long Trail probably has the most straightforward logistics, at least if arriving by car. There are multiple hotels in Williamstown, Massachusetts near the starting point that allow long term parking. Another option is to park near the Amtrak station in Springfield, MA and take Greyhound to Williamstown. That option can simplify the return trip. From Williamstown hotels it is a short cab ride or a tolerable walk to get to trails leading to the Vermont border and the LT.

Once on the trail, things can be pretty simple. Walk to a shelter; spend the night there. There are over 50 shelters along the trail, an average of five miles apart. Each shelter also has a latrine and a water source in the vicinity, so those "tasks" don't require much thought either. Once you determine a reasonable estimate for the number of miles covered per day, a quick glance at a map or guide will determine the target shelter for the night. Even if camping with a tent or hammock, staying near shelters simplifies the logistics. As the trail gets more difficult on the northern miles, plan on fewer miles per day. You will slow down.

There are numerous towns near the LT. Resupplies can be as simple as reaching a road crossing and hitching a ride to the nearest town with a grocery. I tend to plan my food a bit more and mailed food packages to hotels along the way. None of them charged for the service as I also spent the night there. Other than one establishment losing my box, it worked pretty well. (It's not an adventure if you don't spend a few days living on convenience store packaged food.) There are Post Office options as well. I carried less food on the LT than any other trail as the resupply options were so plentiful.

Because I left the trail for a period of time my return from the end was simple. However, returning to the trail's starting point from the Canadian border can be done, though it may get cumbersome. The Green Mountain Club can provide contacts for possible shuttles along the trail. My plan was to get a ride to the Amtrak station near Burlington, VT; 60 miles from the end of the trail. From there, Amtrak can take you to Springfield, MA. If that's where you left your car, great. Otherwise the Greyhound station is nearby and a bus can return you to Williamstown, MA and the southern end of the LT.

For planning a hike on the LT, a good starting point is the Green Mountain

Club, who manages the trail. Their website, greenmountainclub.org contains great information and updates on the trail. In addition, The Green Mountain Club publishes several pieces that are helpful for the thru-hiker. The <u>Long Trail Guide</u> provides background on the trail and area along with meticulous turn by turn directions. The <u>End to Ender's Guide</u> contains detailed information on nearby towns and resupply options. They also publish a map of the LT that's very helpful while hiking on the trail. All can be purchased at greenmountainclub.org. Also helpful is a Guthook phone App for the trail that uses GPS to place the user on a map or elevation profile. The App also contains details and locations of shelters, campsites, water sources and the like.

For **the Colorado Trail** heading from Denver to Durango, there is a parking lot at the Waterton Canyon Trailhead. The Denver Water Authority manages the lot and long term parking can be arranged through them. For more security, there are also paid storage lots in the area. There isn't public transportation between the trailhead and the Denver Airport. However, contact the Colorado Trail Foundation to discuss possibly arranging a ride.

To plan my daily mileage, water stops and such I carried the Colorado Trail Databook. Guthook also sells a phone App that contains much of the same information along with GPS to locate your position on the trail. The Databook never has any battery issues though. Camping is not restricted to specific sites on the CT and not every spot is mentioned in the Databook. Some of my daily distances were adjusted "on the fly" depending upon what I found and how I felt. Latrines and other restroom options vary from rare to non-existent. Bring a trowel.

Resupply opportunities are not as abundant as the Long Trail, but work in much the same way. Road crossings that lead to a nearby town vary from 50 to over 100 miles apart. For the most part, I mailed packages to Post Offices, though groceries were also available.

Once the trail is complete, there is still a several mile hike/hitch to Durango. There is both air and bus service available back to the Denver area.

There are no fees or permits required to hike the CT. The trail does pass through Wilderness Areas that require a permit, but they are free and self-issued as you enter the area.

Complete information about the trail has been compiled by the Colorado Trail Foundation. Their Guidebook is 300 pages packed with turn by turn information about the trail. Also included is backpacking advice, a history of the trail, flora and fauna and much more. It's a great pre-hike read.

On the trail itself I relied on just The Colorado Trail Databook. This four-ounce guide covered all the details needed on the hike. There are simplified trail maps with mileages and elevations for all needed features such as campsites, side trails, available water and road crossings. Both books and much more information are available at Coloradotrail.org.

Logistically speaking, the **John Muir Trail** is both the simplest and most aggravating trail to hike. It's simple in that there is parking near the trailheads in Yosemite. There is public transportation from the Reno, NV or San Francisco, CA airports right to the parks. There's free bus service throughout the park for those, like me, that had an alternate starting point. There's even bus service from Lone Pine, near Mt Whitney, back to Yosemite.

The aggravating part boils down to one word, permit. You can't thru-hike the JMT without a permit and getting one can be a real challenge. I'm familiar with hiking the trail southbound. Northbound permits and logistics may be easier, though I wouldn't count on it. (In 2016, there is roadwork scheduled for Whitney Portal Road and no long term parking will be available there.)

If you are a south bounder there are several decisions to make. First thing, determine when you want to hike, how many are in your group and what specific trailhead you intend to start from. By the way, decide that 24 weeks before you want to go. Now fill out an application. Information is online at http://www.nps.gov/yose/planyourvisit/wpres.htm. Got it? Now find a fax machine and send in that application.

By the end of the day, you will find out if you secured a permit. You probably did not. Per the National Park Service website, over 97% of all applications are denied. Prepare to repeat the process the next day with a new starting date and start location options. One hiker I met on the trail had been denied 22 times before she received a permit to start at Happy

Isles Trailhead, the popular start of the JMT.

Now I fully understand the National Park Service's position. They have a duty to protect the wilderness from overuse and want to provide a true wilderness experience for those that do receive a permit. I certainly did not want to hike the JMT like I was in a conga line or a parade. Based on my experience, allowing 45 people daily to travel over the JMT's first pass seemed like a reasonable number. While I saw others at times, it was not constant and I was always able to find a good spot to camp. None of that makes getting the permit any easier, however. You'll need to plan ahead, yet be very flexible.

There are some permits that are released on site at the park the day before the start date. For someone traveling thousands of miles to hike, that seemed a bit risky to me.

For the non-purist, there are other possibilities. Despite trying for a starting date very late in the season, (after Labor Day) I was turned down repeatedly. After those unsuccessful attempts to secure a permit starting at Happy Isles, I applied for and received a permit to head south from Tuolumne Meadows, about 20 miles down the trail from Happy Isles. This actually worked out very well for me. Before starting my major hike, I arrived at Yosemite a couple days early. I took the opportunity to walk from Tuolumne Meadows to Happy Isles as a day hike. Certainly 20+ miles is a long day hike, but with a 6,000 foot drop in elevation over that stretch, it was very doable. Free bus service through the park assisted with the logistics. While not the way most people hike it, day hiking much of Yosemite "backwards" enabled me to walk the entire trail despite not being able to get a permit from either endpoint.

Resupply on the JMT is interesting and can be costly. Tuolumne Meadows has a Post Office for packages, a restaurant and groceries available. At 61 miles in, Red's Meadow Resort has the same, though there is a fee to hold packages.

Vermillion Valley Resort (90 miles in) has rooms, showers, restaurant and grocery. For a fee, they also hold resupplies sent in five gallon buckets via UPS.

Muir Trail Ranch (110 miles in) holds five gallon buckets for a steep fee

($75 in 2016). In their defense, getting buckets to the location is difficult and involves off road travel. Lodging is minimal and expensive.

Further south, there is no easy resupply. There are no road crossings so a quick hitch into a town is not an option. It either involves a long hike off the JMT and hitchhiking or paying very high prices to have a resupply delivered by pack horse or mule. Don't forget, all your food has to fit into that bear canister too.

On the trail I carried the JMT Pocket Atlas by Blackwoods Press. In addition, I had downloaded the Guthook JMT Trail App onto my IPhone. Both worked well at pinpointing water, campsites and the like. Even hiking during a drought, water was plentiful throughout the trail. Don't forget, there are no shelters to stay in.

Miscellaneous

There are other considerations as well. Time constraints can be a major issue. In round numbers, I spent two weeks on the JMT, three on the LT and five on the CT. Depending upon your location, travel time can be substantial as well. A plus with the CT and LT is that the schedule can be adjusted right up to the last minute as advance permits aren't required.

If one of the aims of the hike is to get away from it all; the Colorado Trail had the fewest people, at least away from towns. There were several days when I was more likely to see a marmot on the trail than another person.

High country hiking buddy

On the other hand, some people hike for the social experience. For them, the shelters on the Long Trail provide a daily gathering spot to interact. When I started the LT in August, it was by far the busiest of the three. On the southern section of the LT, where it shares a path with the Appalachian Trail, be prepared for full shelters by bringing a tent or hammock.

The social center of the Long Trail

If your shelter of choice happens to be a hammock, the Long Trail makes life simpler. There are some long stretches of trail without a flat spot for a tent, but there's nearly always some trees handy. On both the JMT and CT, there are times when stretching a hammock between trees becomes pretty tough. In some higher elevations, there are simply no trees.

Elevation is a real issue to consider. The highest point on the Long Trail is 4,393 feet above sea level on Mt Mansfield. By contrast, the Colorado Trail averages over 10,000 feet in elevation. The highest point on the trail is over 13,000 feet. The JMT reaches the highest elevation in the continental United States, 14,505 feet at the top of Mt Whitney. At that point, there is less than 60% of the oxygen available than there is at sea level. When climbing, that missing 40% is more than noticeable. While there is some acclimation over time, I felt the effects of altitude whenever I was over 9,000 feet or so.

While oxygen deprivation is not an issue on the Long Trail; it more than makes up for it in the ruggedness of the path. Both the JMT and CT were designed and built to be traversed by horses. The LT made no such provisions. There are ladders to climb up and down and several spots where I wished there were ladders. At times the trail surface was a rock called Schist and significantly slipperier than anything on the other trails. After rains the famous boot-sucking "Vermud" reared its ugly head. It's no surprise that despite being at a less stressful elevation, my miles per day progress was lowest on the Long Trail.

The available hiking season is quite similar for the three trails. Per the Colorado Trail Foundation, thru-hikers should hike the CT between mid to late June and late September. If starting from Durango, wait until July. The Pacific Crest Trail Association pegs the JMT season as July through September. The longest availability is for the Long Trail. The Green Mountain Club notes that trails on Vermont State Lands are closed in the spring until Memorial Day Weekend. The "mud season" returns to the LT by late October.

So again, which one?

I believe I could make a compelling case to hike any one of these three trails. Each is different and each has challenges and rewards well worth experiencing.

That being said; if you plan to hike just one long trail in your life, my recommendation is to hike the John Muir Trail. It packs the most incredible scenery into the shortest distance. Wildlife is hugely variable, but I saw the most on the JMT. The permit process can be a pain, but seemed to work out on the trail. There were other hikers around for some level of interaction, but the trail never seemed crowded. There was some rain and a bit of snow on my hike, but the area lived up to its title of The Gentle Wilderness.

If you are looking for big mountain scenery, enjoy being completely self-sufficient and have the time to hike nearly 500 miles, the Colorado Trail might be your hike. There's enough of a build up to somewhat acclimate to the altitude. There were amazing wildflower displays the entire way and the sun shined at least part of every day I was there.

The Long Trail is a good match for those that like the idea of thru-hiking the AT, but can't devote 5-6 months to a trip. The shelters and abundance of hikers very much replicate the social aspect of the AT. Be forewarned though, after 100 miles when the AT and LT split, the challenge level goes up considerably. While I hiked all three trails solo, the rugged hiking and opportunity for injury on the LT made that a risky decision. In this (and many other instances) do as I say and not as I do. Play it smart and don't hike the LT alone.

Perhaps the best way to get a feel for which trail(s) are best for you is to read the following descriptions of my daily life out on the paths. If you've already read my other books about the CT or LT, feel free to skip that section. (Since this is your book now, I guess you really don't need my permission. Read it however you'd like!)

A few words on Safety

No matter which trail, or hopefully all three, you decide to hike, it pays to put some effort into being safe during the hike. However, following the advice in this book, or any book for that matter, cannot guarantee your safety. Some issues are unavoidable, or just bad luck but, a little common sense and planning can go a long way.

The other hikers on the trail are overwhelmingly friendly, like-minded people. Crime on long trails is lower than almost anywhere else you can spend your time. Much of the fear on the trail is fear of the unknown or lack of comfort with backpacking in general.

I have never felt threatened on any trail. However, I also recognize that not everyone is 6' 3" and weighs 185 pounds. Here are a few suggestions that may help you feel better about your safety on the trail.

- Don't make a long trail your first camping trip. Get familiar and confident with all your equipment before heading out.
- Don't backpack alone until you are comfortable being out in nature. There are many backpacking "meet up" groups that enable a new hiker to get experience and confidence in a group setting.
- Bring your cell phone. Coverage continues to get more extensive. You never know when a phone call, or maybe a GPS App, will come in handy. Plus, you need a phone to reserve a hotel room or order a pizza when you get to town.
- Consider a satellite communications device. I carry a Spot Satellite Tracker which is great for both safety and peace of mind for friends and family. The device doesn't need a cell signal and can send text/email messages to selected people along with a Google map of my exact location. Spot can send pre-written messages saying I'm OK or that I need help. In an emergency, the SOS button directly contacts Search and Rescue. However, as they would know my exact location, there's no search; just rescue.
- Trust your gut. If you are interacting with another person and something doesn't seem right, leave the situation. Our instincts have helped us survive for thousands of years, don't ignore them.
- Hopefully this doesn't sound contradictory, but I do typically carry a keychain sized pepper spray while backpacking. My concern is accidently stumbling between a momma bear and her cub, or possibly meeting a wild dog or lovesick moose. However, if it helps you feel better about backpacking around strangers, they only weigh about two ounces. They are legal in most areas, but check before you go. (As with any tool, learn how to use it.)
- Speaking of bears, according to bear.org (North American Bear Center), in the highly unlikely event that a black bear doesn't immediately retreat from human contact, regular pepper spray is

powerful enough to turn the bear around. The giant canisters of "bear spray" are overkill outside of grizzly country.

Fellow camper on the JMT

While on the trail I've met several people that, through lack of preparation, put themselves at risk. I met a man on the trail who was diabetic, nearly out of food and days from a resupply. I don't carry a lot of extra food, but I gave him what I had so he could avoid serious health issues. (When someone just pours a packet of instant oatmeal straight into their mouth, dry; you know they need food.)

One young woman was at the top of Mt Whitney with her hiking boot in pieces. She had started the trail with worn out boots and hoped they would last. She was looking at miles of rough trail in one shoe until I gave her a small roll of duct tape to rebuild her boot.

Those are just a couple examples of where a lack of preparation can have a big impact on both safety and comfort. While not a complete list, here are a few items to think about to assist in your own wellbeing:

- Don't go completely overboard on weight reduction. Bring enough clothes for the expected weather.
- Bring a first aid kit and know how to use it.
- Bring a map and compass and know how to use them together. If the phone dies, that App can't help you.
- All three of the trails in this book pass through black bear habitat. There's no need to be overly concerned, but take appropriate precautions. Keep all food in a bear canister on the JMT and bear bag your food each night on the other trails. Under normal circumstances, common sense will keep you, and the bears, safe. For example, if you don't try to take a selfie with a bear cub, you probably won't need that pepper spray I mentioned before.
- All three trails spend some time above tree line and in the open. Adjust your hiking schedule to minimize being in those areas in the afternoon when the chances of thunderstorms are highest. If a storm comes up, try to get to a lower elevation or find protection quickly.
- If weather conditions are such that's it's dangerous to hike: be it lightening, falling snow on steep, slick slopes or getting too dark to safely navigate; stop. You should have everything you need on your back to wait for better conditions. Use it.
- Common sense and a little caution go a long way toward keeping yourself safe. When you are thinking about doing something risky, also think about how far away help might be.

Part 2, Chapter 4: The Colorado Trail

When I decided to add "Thru-hike" to my bucket list, I considered several options as to which long trail. The length of the Colorado Trail seemed enough to qualify while still being doable. The scenery would be top notch. The weather was historically fairly stable in the summer, without extensive periods of precipitation. Beyond that though, I had one more major reason why I chose to hike the Colorado Trail as my first long thru-hike. I had support nearby. My brother Dan lived within ten minutes of the start of the trail and provided invaluable assistance with logistics. I feel I could have completed the hike without him, but starting the trail was easier with a local base of operation. Plus, knowing he was always ready to assist alleviated many of my concerns. I planned to begin hiking on June 21, the longest day of the year.

One of my concerns was the condition of my feet. I had been diagnosed with a neuroma in my left foot that would eventually result in an operation that involved nerve and bone being removed and titanium being inserted. At the time of the hike though, the treatment was to be padding, cortisone injections and rest. I admit that a 500 mile backpacking trip hardly qualifies as rest so I was even more happy to have my brother's assistance. His help would allow me to ease into the hike and see if the foot would hold up.

Generally, I tend to put up with pain pretty well. I've been told by medical personnel that I "have a high pain tolerance." I've been told by non-medical former friends that I'm "just insensitive." To start the hike, I took twice the recommended dosage of Aleve along with a dose of the wonder drug of the 1960s, Anacin. Beyond that, I hoped that my insensitivity would finally come in handy.

Dan was to drop me at Waterton Canyon, the start of the trail, at 6 AM, drive to parking 17 miles down the trail then start hiking my way till we met. The trail itself began at an altitude of 5,500 feet with 6 easy miles along the South Platte River. The canyon scenery was gorgeous. As I walked the first couple miles, the foot pain settled in to tolerable. Confident I was good for the day, I began to relax and enjoy the beauty.

It wasn't long before the first wildlife sighting as a herd of bighorn sheep makes the canyon its home. With the sun shining and temps in the 60s, my day was looking pretty good.

Once at the end of the canyon, about 6 1/2 miles in, the trail started climbing a bit more steeply through a pine forest into what is known as the Rampart Range. For several miles, switchbacks kept increasing the elevation to a peak of 7,500 feet at about mile 13. Through the higher areas there were views of the taller mountains that loomed in my future.

The foot was holding up, but about this time I began to wonder, "Where the hell is my brother?" (Cell service on the trail is spotty at best.) A mountain biker was stopped along the trail and I asked if he'd noticed anyone walking my way. "What does he look like?"

I replied, "like me but uglier." The biker stated, "Yea, I talked to him a little bit ago. He described you the exact same way." Sure enough we met up shortly thereafter and hiked together down the long decline to the parking lot. We got glimpses of what the next day's hike would hold in store for me, a long climb into the area decimated by 1996 Buffalo Creek

Fire. After nearly eight hours of hiking though, it was time to ice my foot and get a good meal.

Day 2 began with Dan dropping me off at the South Platte River Trailhead, the beginning of Segment 2 (of 28). At that point, the trail was at an elevation of 6,100 feet. It quickly began climbing out of the river valley lush with pine trees into a huge area still scarred from the fire that burned 18 years earlier. Along the way, the trail rose to about 7,800 feet, significantly surpassing the highest point on the Appalachian Trail (6,625 feet). The trail would stay above that mark for the duration of its length.

With the trees burned off, the experience was quite a bit different, but not bad. Wildflowers were abundant. As the miles passed the wildlife began to show itself as well. Far from being desolate, the area contained numerous butterflies, chipmunks, rabbits and deer.

Typical burn area scene

Stopping for a break, the only noise was the breeze on distant mountaintops, at least until some hummingbirds began working nearby flowers and added the propeller like sound of their wing beats. A deep blue sky completed the relaxing scene.

As I neared the end of the day's 11-mile section, I once again met up with my brother. As we neared the car, thunderstorms began forming to the west and were heading our way. Luckily we finished in time to wait out the storm at a local brewpub. The previous two days of mountain hiking followed by a couple beers and a comfortable bed turned out to be a pretty good plan. However, all good things must end and the real work of this trip was ready to begin.

Chapter 5: Reality Begins

My third day began with a longer drive as I was getting further from Denver with each hike. The day was also different as instead of a five pound daypack, I was carrying everything needed to get to Frisco, Colorado, five days and 76 miles distant. Including my food and two liters of water, I had about 31 pounds on my back.

Driving out to the Little Scraggy Trailhead, we passed a bull elk waiting to cross the highway. The animals may have been out, but people were not. Arriving at the trailhead at 6:30, we were the only car. The sky was absolutely clear, but it was only 42 degrees. The pack contained a light fleece and a rain jacket. Perhaps I should have packed a long sleeve shirt.

The trail was void of other hikers as well, but again the scenery did not disappoint. Climbing to still higher elevations, I walked through alpine meadows filled with wildflowers and huge stands of aspen trees. Walking quietly, I startled multiple deer.

Throughout the crystal clear morning, I got numerous views of the still bigger mountains awaiting me to the west. Several still had quite a bit of snow on them. Maybe I really should have packed that long sleeve shirt.

The weather was a repeat of the day before, with thunderstorms building up in the afternoon. There was no brewpub to escape to anymore though. Luckily, I was able to hike into the Lost Creek Wilderness Area as I had planned, set up camp and eat dinner before the lightning and rain started pounding. The temperature dropped fast and lightning was hitting all around as I lay in the tent. I normally use my fleece for a pillow, but instead needed to wear it. An interesting evening to say the least. On the plus side, my foot was staying "tolerable."

As I did every evening while on the trail, I sent a signal back home using the Spot Satellite Tracker. I've mentioned it before, but this is one useful piece of equipment. Without needing cell service, it allowed me to send prewritten messages out to friends or family via email or text, along with a Google map of my location. I had the option of four messages. Mine were variations of, I'm OK, I'm OK and will make it to town tomorrow, I need help, but it's not life threatening (lost or a sprained ankle), and a direct message to Search and Rescue. (A bear is chewing on me or my leg bone is on the wrong side of my skin.) The Spot was well worth the cost and weight (5 ounces), for peace of mind if nothing else.

The morning began with cool and clear weather. The trail started climbing in a hurry, gaining over 1,000 feet of elevation in a couple miles. It was like taking the stairs at a 100 story, with a backpack, and with 30% less oxygen than normal.

On the climb I ran into two other thru-hikers, Eric and Virginia. *(By the way: many of the names of hikers have been changed. This is to protect their identities and/or to hide the fact that I have a terrible memory for names.)*

They planned to skip the section from Kenosha Pass to Salida to avoid any snow. Their plan was to pick up that section later in the summer. Funny how that long sleeve shirt that I did not bring kept entering my thoughts.

After the climb, the trail entered a beautiful wide valley with crystal clear Lost Creek running through it. It was perfect timing as I was running low on water. I was entering the Lost Creek Wilderness area; the first of six. No matter how good water looks, I always filter it just to be safe. After getting the water I followed the trail upstream. A small herd of elk crossed the creek in front of me. I assumed the filter could handle elk pee. The valley continued for several miles and I noticed at least six beaver dams on the creek. I was really hoping the filter handled beaver poo as well.

Lost Creek

The day was going to be a long one as I planned to go 18 miles. I was tired and limping when I arrived at the area I planned to camp. There were only two flat spots around and surprisingly, both were taken, though no one was around. There was nothing to do but keep walking. Hungry as I was, I began eating trail mix while I walked. Not paying attention, I rolled my ankle on a rock and got up close and personal with the ground. Not my best moment. On the bright side, my twisted ankle took my mind off the pain in my foot. As my knee was bleeding, it was time to break out the first aid kit. An alcohol wipe and band aid took care of most of the issue. I'd have to be careful going forward. My skimpy amount of first aid supplies were nearly half gone.

After limping another mile or so, I spotted a small flat area (there are less of them than you would imagine) and called it a day. Total distance for the day was 20 1/2 miles.

After the tough previous day, I was hoping for more of a "bluebird" day.

Ten miles was all I was shooting for. After a short climb through the cool morning air, I was at the bottom of another wide valley. The views were great and I was soon in a huge grove of Aspen, packed full of wildflowers and even bluebirds. The sky cleared to a beautiful deep blue. My foot and ankle were both behaving. As I approached Kenosha Pass, the views of the snow covered peaks in the distance just kept getting better and better. The scene was so beautiful, it took my breath away. It was that or the fact I was at over 10,000 feet.

The trail eventually dropped out of the Kenosha Mountains to the pass at a Forest Service campground. I got to eat lunch at a real picnic table! There was even an indoor toilet. I didn't really need it, but couldn't pass up the opportunity to lighten my load in comfort.

The guidebook stated there was water available in the area, but I couldn't find any. No way they meant the pond I walked by. Since there were only 3 more miles to cover to reach a campsite next to a stream, I decided to head on with about 6 ounces of water left on me.

After a mile of climbing, I was draining the bottle when a woman walked up with a small pack. In response to her question, I mentioned hiking the Colorado Trail. She was very interested and asked quite a few questions. One question I ask her was if there was any water closer than 2 miles. "Why none I'm aware of," she stated while she pulled a full liter of bottled water out of her pack, broke the seal and took a big slug.

That was my cue to cut the conversation short and knock out the last 2 miles. Thunderclouds were building fast over the nearby peaks and it started looking like it would be a photo finish with the rain. Luckily there was just enough time to filter some water, set up camp and be ready to nap through the storm. Seventy-five miles down, 410 to go.

Chapter 6: Up to the Divide

DAY 6 started out cold and clear. At 6 am I began hiking. In 3 miles there was a creek which would be my last chance for water for 11 miles which included a 2,000 foot climb into the Front Range Mountains and the Continental Divide. Just breaking camp at the creek were 2 other thru-hikers, Golden and Wildflower.

Golden was in her early twenties and Wildflower her 50s, but both were accomplished backpackers, having thru-hiked the Appalachian Trail in 2012. We leapfrogged each other up the long grind as the snowcapped mountains I had been seeing for days got dramatically closer. About halfway up (11,000 feet) we began seeing small piles of snow.

By the time we broke above tree line, the piles were no longer small. Long ridges of deep snow blocked the trail and required detours. Luckily, the windswept saddle between two peaks, where we were headed, was free of much snow. Once we reached the divide, the view was unbelievable. It was cold, windy and a hell of a hike to get there, but well worth the price of admission. Little did we know at that point though, that the price for the view was going to be significantly higher than we had already paid.

After several pictures, including celebratory selfies, it was time to start down the west side of the divide. It quickly became evident that getting back down would not be a walk in the park. The trail at that point dropped very little and was cut into the steep mountainside. As we continued, the snow ridges reappeared, then became deeper and more numerous. Each ridge had to be hiked around, over or through, none of which were good options. Several times I was on top of a 4 to 6-foot-tall ridge when the crusty surface would give way and put me instantly ass deep in snow, otherwise known as post holing. Some of the ridges ended with a wall of snow that just had to be ridden down. It was hard enough work that I stayed warm just wearing shorts and a t-shirt.

After a mile or so, we were exhausted and stopped for lunch. Wildflower sat against a tree and I noticed a good size gash in her leg. As she mopped up the blood she talked about how her "country club" friends didn't understand why she liked backpacking so much. "That's true," I remarked. "Some people just don't appreciate how much fun it is to be laying in the snow....on the side of a mountain... bleeding."

Eventually, the snow ridges got smaller and further apart and hiking became normal again. We exchanged small talk and at one point Golden asked what music I'd use to create a sound track for the trail. I mentioned Bob Seger (Roll Me Away), Stephen Stills (Colorado) and of course a big helping of John Denver. That was one of those moments when you realize how far apart experiences are across generations. "Who's John Denver?"

I had actually downloaded several John Denver songs for this very trip, and Golden got to hear Rocky Mountain High and a few others for the first time while actually high up in the Rockies. She said she really liked him, but was possibly just being polite. Hard to tell. We definitely agreed that the views mean much more when you have to earn them like we had.

Eventually we got low enough to reach running water and replenish our supplies. Golden and Wildflower were on a mission to put in more miles to make it into the town of Breckenridge early the next day. I was beat from the day's workout, pulled into the first good looking camp spot and bid them farewell. Apparently though, I set my tent up too close to a squirrel's abode for his liking. As I lay in my sleeping bag writing, he stood just outside the tent chattering at me. It would be a long evening.

Chapter 7: Summertime Snow

The last day of my first week on the trail dawned clear and cool. I had 13 miles to reach the end of Section 6 where's there's a bus stop and a ride to the towns of Breckenridge and Frisco. I had a hotel room reserved in Frisco, but still had some walking to do first. Almost immediately there were more jaw dropping views. A mountain biker rode up and asked if I were a thru-hiker. A yes answer brought a pronouncement that the next section of the trail had 20 feet of snow on it. He then began to quiz me about local history and politics. Despite answering every question with, "I wouldn't know. I'm from Cincinnati," the interrogation continued. Eventually I changed my answer to, "have a good ride," and moved on.

Over the next few miles I met a few other hikers coming the other way. All asked if I were a thru-hiker. Apparently it was becoming obvious. I wondered, was it the confident walk? The filling out of the neck beard? The smell? Hmmm.

There were still 8 miles to go when I spotted Frisco down in a pretty valley, but it was reason enough to pick up the pace. My main obstacle, besides the distance, was walking through areas where the pine bark beetle infestation was being treated. By treated, I mean every tree for acres was cut down and chipped up. When walking these stretches, I put a good dent in my sunscreen supply.

Luck was on my side as a bus and I arrived at the stop at the exact same time. Not ten minutes later I was checking into the Snowshoe Inn on Main Street in Frisco. It's the perfect location, right at a bus stop and within 100 yards of a Laundromat and the Silverheels Bar and Grill (spring for the crab stuffed trout). A glance in the mirror was a bit surprising. While I hadn't been overly hungry on the trail, it was obvious that I'd already lost ten pounds or so. I needed to cram in the calories while in town.

My brother Dan drove down and we planned to take advantage of the great bus service to day hike or "slack pack" (walk without my tent, sleeping bag, etc.) the next section.

The day dawned cloudy and cold and became "the worst hike ever." Dan and I planned to get started early on my slack pack of Segment 7. We grabbed a quick breakfast at the only place open in Frisco at 6 am,

(Starbucks) and drove up to Copper Ski Resort, where the section ended. Because this 14 mile section crested the Tenmile Mountain Range close to its finish, we decided to hike it backwards. This gave us the benefit of tackling the tough, uphill climb first, while we were fresh, and more importantly, get us out of the higher elevations earlier, in case of afternoon thunderstorms.

The hike started at nearly 10,000 feet and immediately began an unrelenting climb from there. We were heading for 12,500 feet, the highest of the trip so far and the trail appeared to be in a hurry to get us there. As we climbed in altitude, the breeze picked up as well. The occasional glimpse of the mountaintops looked intimidating. After about 3 miles, we broke past tree line and lost our protection against the ever strengthening wind. On nearly every day of the trip to this point, early morning clouds would quickly dissipate, but not this day. There would be no sun to warm us up.

For the last two miles before the high point, the area is considered to be tundra. Nothing of any size can grow in the harsh environment so there in no protection from the elements. I was getting hungry and thirsty, but there was no way it was worth stopping. The temperature was down around freezing and the wind had to be at least 50 mph. We looked like a scene from the Weather Channel's Storm Report. The only positive to the situation was there was little snow to deal with. It had all been blown off the mountain.

Eventually we were able to reach the high point and just enough beyond to get a little protection from the wind. Though we had enough warm clothing, neither of us had brought gloves (it was nearly July) and our hands were suffering. Dan's shoe became untied, and he was unable to take care of it. My hands were a little better and so I was able to tie it for him. It did take several tries to get my zipper back up after taking a leak, however. Thankfully Dan didn't have to go, because there would be no help forthcoming.

The other interesting news was that I figured out where all the snow went that had been blown off the other side of the mountain. We were going to have to descend through a winter wonderland.

The trail began dropping by being cut at an angle into the steep mountainside. Large areas were covered by snowfields that alternated between icy (think bobsled run) and soft enough to drop into it crotch deep. Needless to say, progress was slow. In spots where the trail was covered, we also had to guess where it actually was, and look to pick it up at the next clear area. Dan and I did a bit of reminiscing through here. "Remember how we would want to go fishing or canoeing on the very first day of spring? Dad would say, 'You guys are always rushing the season.' You think he might have had a point?"

"Nah."

Eventually we made it to tree line, where things should get better, but not here. The snow covered everything, so there was no way to know where the trail was. The many meltwater creeks were running underneath the snow, so there was the added possibility of dropping through the snow into some mighty chilly water.

There were some footprints in this softer snow, so we followed those for a while; until they stopped. And that was a bad feeling. Miles from the finish. No one else around. No trail. No indication of a trail. The final fall back was my GPS where I had downloaded some waypoints of the trail. The next waypoint was a half mile away so we just plowed in that general direction until we were close to it. The next waypoint was another half mile away so we repeated the process. By then there were some bare spots on the ground and we picked up the trail again. Once Dan got all the ice out his shoes, we were merrily strolling down the trail, only 6 miles to go. The sun even came out!

Just so things wouldn't be too easy, with about two miles to go, we hit another area where all the trees had been cut to fight the pine bark beetle. The work had decimated the trail and once again we were cross country orienteering with the GPS.

Once we made the bus stop it was straight to the Backcountry Brewery. Time for an easy decision: take a day off!

After a relaxing day in Frisco my return to the trail started clear and cool. It actually stayed sunny all day. The next section of trail also climbed to well over 12,000 feet, so it was going to be another day with snow. The Colorado Trail Foundation's website had listed the previous two segments as passable. Today's section was listed as heavy snow; not a word about passable. Back on my own, I climbed out of the Copper Mountain ski resort, spotting snow at an elevation of 10,400; not a good sign. However, some ptarmigans and deer gave me something else to think about.

Soon there was a repeat of the previous days with ridges of snow that had to be climbed over or plowed through. It was looking like a long day until I hit tree line, where there was a surprising absence of heavy accumulation. The occasional snow field was crusted over enough, that, at least for the moment, I could walk on it rather than post hole. A couple snowfields did get the heart rate up in that large creeks disappeared into them. I knew if the snow gave way and dropped me into the creek, it would not be pretty.

By the time I reached the first pass at nearly 12,000 feet, I was ready for an early lunch. Sitting on some rubble enjoying yet another jaw dropping landscape I had the feeling I was not alone. One by one, marmots began popping out of the rocks all around me. Startle one and you'll know why they have the endearing nickname of "whistle pig."

Afternoon brought more snowfields to cross. It was amazing how quickly the tundra wildflowers followed the melting snow. There were often blooming flowers where there had to be snow just a day or two before. After over three miles in heavy snow above 12,000 feet, the trail finally headed down to a more reasonable 10,000 where I set up my tent alongside a rushing stream known as Cataract Creek.

A couple hours later, who shows up but Golden and Wildflower. They had started their day about 2 miles behind me but hiked the extra distance to catch up. They are some serious hikers.

For dinner, Golden told me she had a bag of scrambled eggs from the hostel they stayed in two nights ago and offered me some. "They're green!" I replied when I spotted her offering. "That's the avocado," she stated. "It has some vegetarian ham in it too."

Despite still being hungry after my freeze dried entrée; from somewhere deep in the recesses of my mind I remembered that I should not and could not eat green eggs and ham. I declined the offer.

I thought I heard a bear in camp during the night, but apparently it was Golden finding out that green eggs and ham weren't a good idea for her either. She and Wildflower were planning on hitching a ride into Leadville for food of a different color. I'd planned on a 20-mile day and so packed up and headed out early under a clear blue sky.

Much of the trail through this area was on old Forest Service roads. It was a tad boring, but the miles were easy. Along the way, an older couple walked towards me and asked about some side trails. I was not much help, but showed them my maps. After a short "domestic" they turned around and started hiking with me, back the way they came. They were pretty interesting to talk to and were the stereotypical couple that had been together so long they began to resemble each other. They talked alike, dressed somewhat the same and even had matching sideburns.

The easy miles ended abruptly when I got to the Holy Cross Wilderness Area. In a mile I climbed close to 1,000 feet and was back over 11,000. (It felt more like the "Holy Crap" Wilderness Area.) I had hoped because I remained a bit lower than yesterday, that there'd be no snow to contend with. Man, was I ever wrong. It was back to plowing through drifts and post holing. Despite having waterproof shoes, there was no way to avoid wet feet for 3 of the last 4 days, and it was starting to take a toll. No one has ever said to me, "Your feet look pretty," but they've rarely looked as nasty as they did then. I stopped a couple times to attempt to dry my socks in the sun, but eventually the only thing that improved the situation was taping over the blisters with duct tape. That actually helped quite a bit. After 20 miles for the day though, I was pretty much worn out. I set up camp near a small pond, but still at an elevation of 11,000 feet. The sky was clear. The campsite was partially covered in snow. A chilly night was in the cards. On the plus side, mosquitos, which had become surprisingly troublesome, were rendered too cold to fly.

Chapter 8: A Family Break

Day 12 started like nearly every day, cool and sunny. Despite temperatures that put a bit of frost on the tent, I had slept well.

Soon after leaving the Holy Cross Wilderness, I entered the Mt Massive Wilderness area. Much of the day was spent in heavy pine forest with just an occasional glimpse of the rightly named Mt Massive. At 14,421 feet tall, it's a few feet shorter than nearby Mt Elbert, tallest in the state, but appears to be a bigger rock.

My brother Bob had flown out to visit and he and Dan walked towards me from the other end of the segment. With 4 miles left in a 16 mile day, we met up. It was great to see them. Even better, Bob shouldered my pack the rest of the way to the car.

First we drove to the Twin Lakes General Store to pick up a box I'd mailed to myself. Other than looking like it had been kicked from Cincinnati to Colorado, it was fine. The box contained all my food for the next section along with a few travel sized "consumables" such as sunblock, toothpaste and contact lens solution.

After checking in at the Leadville Super 8, it was off to the Golden Burro bar and grill. We all got bean burritos, very tasty and filling. However, they should not be served to anyone over 65; at least not if you share a motel room with them.

The next day's effort was almost like taking a day off. We hiked a short (12 mile) section that's relatively flat and the best part was my brother Bob carried a daypack with everything we might need for the day. I carried absolutely nothing and felt like I was floating. Dan walked with us for the first mile or so, then headed back to the car so he could meet us near the end of the day's hike.

Mt Elbert

With no pack and easy conversation, the miles flew by. The scenery alternated between conifers and huge groves of aspen, with occasional glimpses of Mt Elbert and Massive. After about six miles we started seeing Twin Lakes. Despite its name, there's really only one lake that just gets narrow in the middle. Regardless, it was a pretty sight as we dropped out of the woods to walk along the bank. You'd think that would be an interesting section, but it was 4 miles long with absolutely no shade. By then, it was around noon and the sun began to roast me through the sunscreen.

With about two miles of lakeshore to go, Dan came walking up with a hiker he had met. Marvin was another thru-hiker that skipped the snow area and was hiking back toward it. The snow had been melting fast, but Marvin still had some work in front of him.

The afternoon job for me was the Laundromat, though I can't say the washing got my socks to smell fresh. Much better, but not fresh. That evening, it was back to the Golden Burro, though no one was allowed the get burritos. After buffalo burgers all around, there was still time to find a TV and watch the Rockies lose another ball game. All in all, a great change of pace. I was 180 miles deep into the hike.

Chapter 9: Wishing

On the last day of my second week on the trail, sunny and warm of course, I was back to hiking on my own. Dan and Bob drove me back to where we had stopped the day before, helped me on with my pack and left me with words of encouragement. Even though I've always known it, it's nice to be reminded how much they care.

Walking along Twin Lakes first thing in the morning I got some tremendous views of the mountains reflected in the water. Soon however, it was time to start climbing.

Part of the route was along Forest Service Roads and through their camping areas, which are pretty basic. Due to the Independence Day holiday, they were fairly crowded though. As I was walking through, a guy ran up and asked if I were a thru-hiker. When I said yes, he told me I was off the trail. He stated I probably missed the turn about 100 feet back because, "those assholes are camped right on the trail."

I walked back with the guy and sure enough, there was the trail, right between a big wall tent and some bike trailers. As I thanked him and turned to leave, his wife/girlfriend came up offering me a banana, some juice and to take my trash. Now that's pretty friendly.

After walking a few more miles of Forest Service roads, I began to drop into the Clear Creek Valley. In stark contrast to the forests I'd been walking through, this hillside, with a full southern exposure, only supported scrub growth and even some small cacti. Of course, to be consistent with everywhere else I'd been on the trail, the cacti were in bloom.

As I ate lunch by the creek, a day hiker walked by and asked about my hike. After a few minutes he offered me some water. He didn't appear to believe me when I pointed at the creek and said I had plenty.

After lunch I started on the first of several major climbs to be "conquered." Climbing close to 3,000 feet over 4 miles slowed progress to a crawl. Worse yet, short rain showers were hitting about every half hour, forcing me to put on and take off rainwear several times.

As I finally arrived where I had planned to camp for the night, it began to sprinkle. Rather than rush to put up the tent, I thought I'd wait out another "short" shower, then set up. A half hour later, I was still standing under a pine tree watching the pouring rain turn my chosen spot into a quagmire. After an hour and a half, a short break in the rain lasted just long enough to throw up the tent and pile everything, including myself, inside to wait out the next downpour. The weather finally cleared at dark. It made for a late dinner. You'd think freeze dried sweet and sour pork would be worth the wait, but it's not.

I'm sure some people think that backpacking for 500 miles is pure, unadulterated fun. Those people would be wrong. Actually, for the most part they are right. There are times though when they are very wrong. Besides the sheer effort of hauling yourself, and everything thing you need to be comfortable (or at least survive) through high altitude mountainous wilderness, you also have the weight of any doubts, fears and unhappiness that you drag along. Not always being a "glass half full" guy results in the figurative weight I carry getting fairly significant at times. However, it isn't tough to handle when the sun is shining and the views are great. When they're not though, conditions can get you wishing that the hike was over.

Sore tired legs, tasteless meals that don't satisfy and having to crap in a hole you just dug are difficulties that you accept in exchange for beautiful surroundings and a tremendous feeling of accomplishment. It's generally a pretty good trade, but not always. Hours of rain can wash out whatever positive emotion you woke up with. You wish the sun would come out, but it doesn't. You wish for a worthwhile view, but rain and fog restricts your sight and dampens your spirit, clothes and equipment. When the rain eases up, the mosquitos come out. With nothing positive to occupy your mind, it starts to wander to things you shouldn't dwell on; the knee that is starting to hurt, the taste of this morning's freeze dried eggs. You relive old relationships, wishing you could change things you did wrong.

Eventually, you leave the past and just start wishing for a better here and now. By the end of the day things get pretty simple. You wish only for dry clothes, a cold beer and a warm place to take a dump. However, what you have is a wet tent and you're 3 days away from the closest hotel. As you lay in your smelly, damp sleeping bag, you wish the hike was over, but it's not.

At times like these, rather than quit, you need to fight the negativity. For some, a positive childhood memory will do the trick. I think of my dear old Mom's favorite saying. She used it often when, as a young boy, I would tell her about what I wanted for dinner or just something I wished for. I can almost hear her now. "Wish in one hand and crap in the other; see which one fills up first."

With warm memories of childhood floating through my head, I drifted off to sleep. 300 miles to go.

Chapter 10: Prediction? Pain

Reporter: *Clubber, what's your prediction for the fight?*
Clubber Lang (as poignantly played by Mr. T in Rocky 3): *Prediction? Pain.*

Now there's no way to write about being in the Rockies without, at some point, tying it into the Rocky movie franchise.

Now there have been times in the past when competing in running races, triathlons or other sports where I felt I could beat another opponent. I've even felt I could "beat" a course I was familiar with. Five hundred miles of the Rocky Mountains is a different story. If you try to beat the mountains, as Clubber said, you just get pain. Or, as Adrian screeched at Rocky as he was headed to Moscow to fight the big Russian, "You can't win!" (By the way, thanks for the support there, Adrian.)

The Rocky Mountains cannot be beaten. They are too tall, too vast and have the staying power of....hell, a mountain.

For the first two weeks of this trip, I was "winning." I had created a schedule to follow and was not only meeting it, despite various foot/ankle injuries, I was beating it.

Apparently, it was time for the mountains to bring me back to reality. I was hiking into the Collegiate Mountains. After packing up a wet camp from the previous night's rain, I was looking at two huge climbs. Straight from camp there was a 1,400 foot climb that took me near 12,000 feet onto Mt Harvard. Between the wet camp the night before, the climb and the intense sun above tree line, I was already feeling worn out and it was only 9 am.

After a short drop, it was back up Mt Columbia and a couple community college peaks as well. A long downgrade had me having a late lunch down around 9,000 feet. There were some nice camping spots there, but my schedule had me getting past Mt Yale yet that day. The climb was the steepest I'd yet encountered and I was suffering with every step. Yale's entrance exam was more than I could handle and the mountain may have discovered my "Achilles Heel." Ironically enough, that was my Achilles tendon, which was hurting worse with each step.

As I struggled up the cliff disguised as a trail, I met a woman and her dog heading down. She asked if I was a thru-hiker (had to be the neck beard) and we talked about the trail. When I mentioned how steep the trail was at that point, she cheerfully replied, "Oh, it gets steeper!"

Unbelievably, it turned out that she was right. As I walked, it was like I was face to face with the trail. At this point I finally decided that I needed to stop trying to meet an arbitrary schedule and just take what the mountains would give. Thankfully what the mountain gave me was a beautiful alpine meadow about halfway up Yale. A stream was nearby, but far enough away to not draw mosquitoes. A small grove of pine protected a flat area just right for the tent, but left in enough breeze to dry yesterday's rain off the material. I had plenty of time to take a nap and enjoy the evening. The weather was gorgeous and I was able to relax and recharge. The world was a much better place than it had been just a few hours earlier. It turned out to be better to enjoy nature, rather than compete with it.

Also on the site was an old abandoned cabin. It seemed rather symbolic of the mountain's infinite patience. The cabin was about halfway back to being reabsorbed by the mountain and Mt Yale had all the time in the world to finish the project.

Chapter 11: Closing in on Halfway

The morning started off, you guessed it, sunny and cool. After a short, but hard grind to the high point on Mt Yale, there was a sharp downhill, then rolling terrain for over 20 miles. It looked like a day to get in some decent mileage. Starting out, my Achilles tendon even felt fine. Hopefully, that was a one-time occurrence. The sky stayed mostly clear throughout the morning and I was coating myself with sunscreen by 8 am. Not only was much of the trail that day in the open, what woods it traveled through were relatively thin. Considering that the sun's intensity at 10,000 feet is 50% stronger than at sea level, it doesn't take long to figure out that sunscreen is a real necessity on the trail.

After settling in to a shady spot for lunch, I apparently was once again irritating a squirrel. As he chattered at me, I pulled out the camera to get a shot of him. He in turn continued to get closer. It seemed cute until he kept closing in and started baring those tiny little buck teeth. At the same time, it appeared his nest mate was executing a flanking maneuver to block my escape. I decided that I had enough squirrel pictures and it was time to move on.

There must be some problems getting a trail corridor near the town of Mt Princeton. The trail dumped onto a Forest Service road, then through a private "dude ranch" and finally onto paved roads for nearly 6 miles. (This was actually the only road walking on the entire trail.) A saving grace of that desolate stretch was walking right by (and into) the Mt Princeton Hot Springs Country Store. I took a short snack break that included a Hot Pocket made my usual way (still frozen on one end and nuclear hot at the other), cheese, yogurt, a quart of ice cream and some pop. Hopefully that would tide me over till dinner. My appetite had really kicked in over the last few days and I was constantly hungry. Back on the trail at the far side of town, there was a sharp climb and I ended the day overlooking the town with a great view of the chalky white cliffs of Mt Princeton and the surrounding hills. I had made it through the Collegiate Peaks!

Dry camp near Mt Princeton

Surprisingly enough, day 17 started off clear and warm. As I left town the night before, I grabbed 2 1/2 liters of water from Chalk Creek that was to last through dinner, breakfast and 6 1/2 miles of trail. Between the dry air, intense sun and hilly terrain, I might have underestimated my liquid requirements. I read somewhere that, when drinking enough, healthy urine is clear. Mine reminded me of orange juice. At least it was pulp free. Orange juice is healthy, isn't it? Regardless, I spent quite a bit of time filtering and drinking water at the first creek I reached.

The stretch alternated between open land and young forest. The trail itself was relatively level. Relatively is the operative term here; this is the Rocky Mountains. During the 19 miles walked this day, I climbed and dropped over 7,000 feet in elevation. Through the day I was close to deer, rabbits, turkeys (with young), and what I think were quail. No more vicious squirrels though. What did get a bit vicious was the weather. By early afternoon thunderstorms were building over the nearby mountaintops. Quickly they spread, any blue sky disappeared and the rain began. It looked ugly and by the time I put on a rain jacket, pants and a pack cover, (yes, the pack has its own rain jacket) the rain began in earnest. The rumble of thunder was almost constant when the hail started. Luckily the hail stayed somewhat small. Big enough to tell when it hit, but not big enough to hurt. With nothing better to do, I kept walking. Apparently that type of weather has no impact on elk, as a female just stood there and stared as I walked by.

After an hour or so the rain let up and I was closing in on my goal for the day, where the trail crosses Rt. 50. It was there that I had a cab pick me up and take me to nearby Salida for another day off. I was 252 miles deep into the trail; officially past halfway!

Chapter 12: A New Family is Born

Since many thru-hikers use hostels to save a few bucks, I thought I'd try a night at the Simple Hostel in Salida while I took a day off. As I was a Hostel Virgin (sounds like a band I could have been in when I was 16), I thought I'd ease into it by getting a private room. It's definitely a different experience. A guy in the living room was playing the guitar. I didn't know the song so I headed onto the porch and had some interesting conversations with a few hikers there. I was the only guy with a beer in his hand. I was also the only guy without a joint in his hand. (It was Colorado after all.) Eventually, I met a hiker called White Pine who was thru-hiking the CT and was a day ahead of me.

The hostel was an interesting experience and handy for getting a supply box I had mailed to myself at the Post Office. As I was meeting Dan the next morning to hike another section with him, I kept walking out to the Super 8 and got us a room. I received a text from Golden and Wildflower saying they were in Salida, wondering where I was. I shared the plan to slack pack and they were all for joining us.

It was clear in the morning as we walked Segment 15 backward, again getting the higher elevations over with earlier in the day. About halfway, we passed White Pine, who was heading the other way. We stopped at Monarch Crest for lunch which may have been most beautiful spot to that point.

Monarch Crest

After watching the clouds build, we started down in a hurry but not fast enough. Rain and hail started when we were about halfway down from the crest. By the time we got back to Salida however, it was clear again. Dropping the ladies back at the Hostel, Dan and I tried Moonlight Pizza, Wall Bangers and eventually Amicas, which has some great lasagna (I get hungry). It was there we met up with Golden and Wildflower for dinner.

On day 20 (who'd have guessed, clear weather) Dan dropped off Golden, Wildflower and me at the trailhead. We were looking at a 20 mile day to get to Baldy Lake to camp.

One issue for women hikers is guys that try to attach themselves to them or their group through the hike in the hopes romance might bloom in the woods. The situation is common enough on the Appalachian Trail that it has a name, Pink Blazing. Not wanting to be seen as a Pink Blazer, I told them to feel free to move on without me. (There's no doubt they could both out-hike me if they wanted,) They wouldn't hear of it. In fact, Golden began calling us The Family.

There was also some discussion of trail names. Most, but not all hikers have a trail name. About half name themselves and the others are named. Somewhere I had read about a woman on the AT that did not yet have a trail name. In the middle of the night she was awakened by stomach cramps, but rather than going out into the dark to relieve herself, had decided to stay in her tent and make use of a Ziploc bag. Things did not go well and in the morning she had a new, rather unflattering trail name. I decided to name myself rather than leave my trail title to fate. ("After the bear attack we just started calling him Lefty.")

The problem is, I already have about 20 names. Ask anybody named James. Besides Jim there's Jimmy, Jim Bob, Jimbo, Jiminy, and so on. It's hard to keep up with. I needed something I could remember. I did however, have one non-James related nickname when I was little. My brother Bob named me after Tarzan's pet lion in the old movies, Simba. Even though I hadn't used it in decades and Disney added a little too much cuteness to it, it beat getting named after a lapse in judgement. Simba it became.

By the time we (mainly me) struggled the full 20 miles to Baldy Lake to camp, there was somebody else already there, none other than White Pine. He had a fire going and we all gathered around it that evening. By morning, the Family Meeting on the day's hiking plan had four in attendance. The Family now had representatives from Georgia, Mississippi, Iowa and Ohio, all the big mountain states.

Chapter 13: Cow Country

Leaving Baldy Lake was the start of yet another long day. After starting out clear, we walked through multiple bouts of rain. Golden found a can of peaches along the road and, forgetting the green egg fiasco, ate them. We'll see how that goes... Later that day she saw that someone had dumped some trail mix into the road's cattle guard ditch and spent several minutes working on a plan to fish it out before being convinced to move on. I believe she needed to consider packing more food.

That's right though, we were getting into cattle country, mostly rolling land that had been leased out for grazing. The travel was a bit easier and we covered 22 miles that day; with total mileage passing 300.

Beginning my third week on the trail, I was greeted by yet another clear sunrise. The cow country continued in earnest. Rolling hills, going through gates on a regular basis, plenty of cow pies all over. I wasn't in a big rush to drink water from a creek surrounded by cow crap, but was starting to run low. Then a huge bit of trail "magic." At around three miles into the day's hike through a long stretch with no shade was a silver dome tent and a horse trailer. They were set up by a trail angel called Apple. The horse trailer was set up for sheltered sleeping and the dome had coolers full of ice cold pop, Gatorade and water. Coffee and a gas stove to heat water were there too. Quite the treat. I dumped out the filtered cow poop water I already had and filled up with clean stuff.

Just after lunch we were at the start of a 2 1/2-mile-long open valley when the afternoon thunderstorm decided to unload on us. There was some fear about lightening but I stated there was no way the lightning would bypass the mountaintops and strike us. I actually told Golden, a former lifeguard, that she was more likely to fall in the nearby creek and drown than be hit by lightning. Amazing how when you say something with confidence, people will believe it. It was a tough stretch for Golden as she was not only afraid of being killed by lightning, she also had an unnatural fear of being trampled by cows. And we had to split a herd to get up the valley. At one point, we even had to walk around a dead cow. Luckily, it didn't appear to have been hit by lightning, or I'd have lost all credibility.

At the end of the valley, the bridge over the Cochetopa Creek was out and I got to use my sandals I'd carried for 300 miles. Creek crossings are just one example of how well the trail is designed and maintained. After crossing literally dozens of creeks and streams of all sizes, mostly swelled by snowmelt, this was the first crossing that I had to get my feet wet.

We ended up walking 20 miles and cows and cow pies were with us nearly the whole way. They were even in the La Garita Wilderness area, which was a sad surprise. (That section became known as the La Giardia Wilderness.) However, considering the steepness of the trail, I had a new respect for a cow's balance and hiking ability. Climbing into the La Garita Mountains we eventually got clear of the cow area and camped in a beautiful spot about 26 miles from Lake City. I was able to make my water last till then. Once again, I only had to worry about drinking elk and beaver poop.

The Family was set to break up, however. White Pine was shooting to climb a 14,000-foot mountain in the morning (San Luis Peak), then head into Creede for a resupply. Golden and Wildflower were ready to walk some huge miles in an effort the get to Lake City for their own resupply as they were nearly out of food. There just weren't enough canned goods lying along the road to fulfill their needs. Just before the big breakup though, we received our second trail magic in one day.

As we walked by one of the trail's access points, we met a woman who was cutting her thru-hike attempt short. Her family was picking her up and we stopped to chat. Suddenly they began pulling out her unused trail food and insisting we take it. There was enough for everyone to make it to Lake City without huge miles or swinging into Creede. Happily, the Family would stay together a while longer. Yet another 20-mile day.

My hike's 23rd day started clear and cold. We began at around 6 AM with a long walk up a beautiful valley. The early start was due to much of the day being above tree line and the recent daily thunderstorms. The three previous big mileage days had taken their toll on me and I was dragging a bit from the get go. The morning consisted of just one hill, but one that was 7 miles long and topped out near 13,000 feet. Before the day was over we dropped and climbed three more times. The hills were killing me and I felt I may be holding the others back. It got me wondering about The Family staying together. I enjoyed the company immensely but considered that I may need to hike at a slower pace. I was keeping an open mind, but thinking I might be better off setting off on my own after Lake City.

As I struggled up to the Continental Divide, I mentioned that when people over 55 die walking to the fridge, it's no longer considered medically untimely. Golden nicely told me I have a long time before I need to worry about that. I mentioned that I was 56. She asked that her last statement be stricken from the record.

The Family at 13,000 feet

After 15 tough miles, we made camp early where I did a little laundry and washed up in the creek. As I hung my wet clothes in a nearby tree, it began to hail. There was some doubt they'd be dry in the morning.

Chapter 14: Lake City and the High Ground

Yet another clear morning and we had 10 miles to hike to get near the town of Lake City. Much of the morning involved a long trek through the high tundra of aptly named Snow Mesa. Even in the middle of July there were still pockets of snow.

As we hiked I met two more hikers, Gimpy and Gristle. They were both around 60 and lived 7 miles from each other in Texas. The funny thing is, they didn't know each other until they'd met on the trail a few days earlier.

The ladies made it to the road first and quickly got a ride into town. Shockingly, it took a bit longer for the 4 guys to get a lift. Five of us with 4 packs crammed into a Kia Rodeo. Three of us sat with packs on our laps in the back seat. The ride is 17 miles downhill and you could smell the brakes overheating just a few miles into the twisted downslope. White Pine buried his head in his pack so he couldn't see. I concentrated on the sticker that warns of the vehicle's high center of gravity and rollover potential as we whipped through the turns. Our ride ended at the edge of town when the driver pulled into the local liquor store. After kissing the ground, it was just a short walk to the center of town and the local motels and hostel.

I headed for Silver Spur Motel while the others all turned into the hostel. After Golden received an inordinate amount of attention at the hostel, the ladies also decided to "upgrade" to a room at the Silver Spur. White Pine had no such issues and decided to stick it out where he was.

Crossing paths later at the local laundry, the ladies were intrigued that I was wearing clean, cotton clothes while feeding quarters into the dryer. Apparently I was the first thru-hiker they knew to think of mailing himself throw away clothing with the rest of the resupply package. Perhaps it would start a trend. Despite mailing food to myself, I needed to load up at the grocery store as well. I'd been constantly hungry on the trail and had lost more weight. I needed to carry more food, pack weight be damned.

One night in town was enough for White Pine and he headed back out on the trail where he'd wait for the The Family to catch up. The rest of us took a zero mileage day to stay in town, relax, eat and even stroll through the arts and crafts fair that closed one of the town's three streets.

While in town I got an update that "the boy," Matt, would be getting home from the Peace Corps a few days earlier than he had planned. In addition, I also saw that two people had been killed and over a dozen hospitalized due to lightning strikes in the higher elevations of Rocky Mountain National Park. The better part of the next 40 miles of the Colorado Trail was over 12,000 feet in elevation.

Between wanting to see Matt as soon as possible and not wanting to spend additional time in the lightning kill zone, my thoughts about slowing down went out the window. I would just work as hard as needed to stay with The Family and put in big miles. They'd been a great group to hike with and I was sure they'd help me along. I'd just need to stay a safe distance from Golden when she used her umbrella during the thunderstorms. Now that I'd settled into the trail name of Simba, I was going to try to stick with that rather than get hit by lightning and have a new name like "Juice," "Twitchy," "Crispy" or "Toast."

After getting a ride from Crazy Mike back to the trailhead for the start of day 26, we were joined by Bob, trail name Bob, who was also thru-hiking. Bob started the same day that I did, but had skipped the snow section, and also had to leave the trail for a funeral.

Thunderstorm on the way

While the day started clear, a massive thunderstorm built quickly and headed right for us. We were in a high open area and made a beeline for a small group of trees. Golden, Wildflower and I set up tents near, but not in, the clump of trees. Bob decided to just go with his raingear. The storm hit with tremendous force. Lightning was hitting all around, the wind was fierce and the rain was coming down in buckets. The only thing that kept my tent from flying away was the pack and I still weighed over 200 pounds total. After about 20 minutes the wind noise dropped just enough that I could yell, "Hey Bob, how's that rain gear working out for you?" I could only hear a partial reply, but I think I heard the words, "wish," and "tent," along with several others I won't repeat here.

Once the storm went through, the temperature dropped significantly and no more storms developed. As we walked ever higher, we came across a herd of sheep being guarded by two very attentive sheep dogs. It was pretty interesting watching them work the herd.

By early afternoon we came upon a yurt where White Pine had waited out the storm. This is one of only a couple possible shelters on the entire trail. As the sky stayed clear, we all decided to risk putting in more miles. Before the day was over, we had climbed to the highest point on the trail, over 13,200 feet. Hopefully the regular afternoon thunderstorms would hold off for another day or two. I was also dealing with more Achilles trouble. Hopefully just another one-day issue.

Chapter 15: Walking the Great Divide

It was cold and clear in the morning, probably about freezing. Five minutes into the day, Bob and I found the trail blocked by two moose. They looked at us, looked at each other, and looked at us some more. The standoff lasted about five minutes before they decided to drop off the trail. It was a good thing as we had nowhere to go if they had decided to charge. Worst case scenario though, I was fairly sure I could outrun Bob.

We spent the entire day bouncing between 12-13,000 feet, mostly along the Continental Divide. Luckily, we caught a real break with nice and clear weather as the whole day was above timberline. I filled up on drinking water from the Rio Grande when it was nothing more than a bit of snowmelt. It was no problem to step across the river and keep my feet dry. There was still significant snow in the spectacular San Juan Mountains. We ended up camping at 12,500 feet, highest of the entire trip. There was no doubt it was going to be a cold night.

Continental Divide in the San Juan Mountains

I woke up to a hard freeze and an iced over tent. I was cold, but not miserable and actually slept pretty good. This might be a good time to explain White Pine's minimalist approach to camping equipment. His sleeping bag was rated for 40 degrees (mine was 23). Instead of a tent, he slept under a tarp. Not just any tarp, but one made out of the clear, thin plastic that is used to cover windows. The stuff that's a little thinner than plastic food wrap (think Saran Wrap). If he got too cold, he built a fire to stay warm. Unfortunately, when camping in tundra well above tree line, there's no wood to burn. Earlier in the trip, he actually had a Snowshoe Hare come in under the tarp to sleep by his feet, warming him a bit. There were no rabbits or marmots to join him that night though. By 3 am, White Pine was out of his cozy tarp, doing calisthenics in an attempt to deal with the sub-freezing temperature. Survival Boot Camp lasted until first light. Thankfully he didn't need music to work out so I slept blissfully unaware of his predicament. I was 395 miles deep into the mountains.

After a short walk through the cloudless high tundra in the morning, the trail followed a narrow ridge between two canyons, then began the long descent through the Weminuche Wilderness down towards the town of Silverton.

The canyon I dropped into literally looked like it was out of a movie. I am not an extraordinarily religious person, but this valley felt like it was carved by God himself. I started the descent on over two dozen switchbacks. The ground was slightly less steep than a cliff, yet it was packed with wildflowers thicker than I'd ever seen in my life.

Once through the switchbacks, the drop continued steeply through a field of boulders and alongside a rushing stream of clear cold snowmelt, joined by more streams and waterfalls all along the way. Across the stream, sheer cliffs towered a thousand feet overhead. The beauty and majesty were enough to put a lump in my throat every time I looked around. I couldn't spend too much time wandering in awe however, as much of the trail was scratched into the side of a cliff where a bad step could have ended my trip for good. And this went on literally for miles. If you are capable of a hard hike at altitude, put Elk Creek Canyon on your bucket list. Neither words nor pictures do it justice.

There is an expression among long distance hikers; "Hike your own hike." One of the things that I thought would make my hike special would be the rare opportunity that presents itself near where Elk Creek empties into the Animas River. At this spot, you can walk out of the woods onto a train track, wave down a steam locomotive, slip the conductor some cash, and ride the train into town. That was an opportunity I was not going to miss! While the others walked the last few miles into Silverton, I "rode the rails" straight out of history and into the scenic mountain village. There I proceeded to eat a half pound hamburger, then a half pound buffalo burger, along with fries and a salad while waiting for their arrival so we could eat. Tasty.

Silverton would be a quick, overnight stop to resupply, then the final stretch into Durango and completion of the Colorado Trail!

Chapter 16: The Final Stretch

As I lay in the tent I could hear the heavy footsteps of the bear as it entered the camp. It began sniffing at my tent and somehow I knew it was a matter of time before it was coming in. Silently I opened the lock blade on my pocketknife and waited. If it was a mature Grizzly, I didn't have a great chance to survive an attack, but if I could just inflict enough damage, maybe it would leave without harming anyone else. "If I save the rest of The Family," I grimly thought, "that wouldn't be a bad way to check out." Just then the massive head tore through the nylon tent wall and the big Grizzly's first bite was to my shoulder....

That's when I woke up back home in Cincinnati as my stupid, stupid cat was clawing my shoulder in an attempt to wake me up. Once the cat (bear) was locked out of the room, I could reminisce in peace about what actually happened on the home stretch of the hike.

After four full weeks on the trail, I still had 75 miles to go. Five of us, The Family and Gimpy, got a ride up to Molas Pass on a sunny Saturday morning. This section of trail was popular with the mountain bikers and we were passed by an actual busload of them. We hit the high pass (12,500 feet) at the same time as a nasty looking thunderstorm, waited about an hour as it slid by, but ended up staying dry for another day. This made for long day as we had trouble finding a good camp site. After 20 miles walked, The Family caught back up with Gimpy who had himself caught up to and set up camp by Bob.

Day 30 was a tough water day. Six of us started out, loading up on water at Straight Creek, 7.5 miles into the day. The next sure water source was 22 miles distant, though we heard from a north bound hiker that there was a small creek in 15 miles. Since his trail name was Pants on Fire, I had my doubts. Each of us carried 3 liters of water, but we would need it all, and more, if we couldn't make it to water that day. The sun was out in force from sunup to sundown. Much of the trail was old Forest Service roads which let in most of the sun's power, drying us out.

The views were still tremendous, so that part stayed great. Our merry band picked up another member when a south bounder that was going to take another week to finish suddenly decided to speed up and stay with "the cool kids table." Casey was a science student and stated he wanted to work at a job that hadn't been invented yet. Hmmm, maybe he'll be a flying car mechanic.

At 7 pm, after hiking 22.5 miles in the blazing sun, we happened across the water supply and a spot to set up 7 tents. You wouldn't think people would be so excited about getting a drink of water out of a small, mossy creek, but when it's the only option, it tastes wonderful. It was the biggest group I'd been with on the entire trail and there was lively conversation around the fire. It was that evening when my dream to hike the Junior Version of hiking's Triple Crown was conceived.

By day 31 things started to wind down. Gimpy and Bob took off early, but The Family only planned to hike about 16 miles, leaving 14 or so to get to the finish in Durango. We recorded the last of Golden's Monday Videos for her blog. This one involved five hikers dancing (poorly) down the trail to the relaxing strains of "We Found Love" by Rihanna. In addition, we still climbed to over 12,000 feet one last time through the La Plata Mountains. I found it hard to believe, but the views continued to get even better.

La Plata Mountains

As we walked a high ridge, a look to the left afforded a view that reminded me of the Smoky Mountains, but more rugged. A glance to the right gave me a view of snow touched majesty that is classic rugged Rocky Mountains. Eventually we dropped down far enough to get back into Aspen trees and camp near a "gurgling" stream.

The last day was spent on a slow drop in altitude down to around 7,000 feet. Although by most standards the scenery remained tremendous, it couldn't compete with the above the tree line views of the previous days. Mostly I walked alone, trying to absorb just a little more of the experience before it ended. By midafternoon, we reached a sign telling us we were done; all five members of The Family had thru-hiked the Colorado Trail. After congratulatory hugs and photos, we began walking towards Durango and its hotels, showers and brewpubs. Luckily we all quickly got a ride.

The Finish!

After cleaning up, The Family met up at Carver's Brewpub in downtown Durango. As promised, they provide a free glass of Colorado Trail, Nut Brown Ale to all thru-hikers. The evening was spent reliving recent memories with great new friends, plates of good food and more than enough beer. The trip had been, in a word, epic; simply epic.

Part 3, Chapter 17: The Long Trail

The spring after I completed the Colorado Trail I was able, after several attempts, to secure a permit to hike the John Muir Trail. I would start that hike right after Labor Day. Between its high elevation and difficult resupply, it was going to be a tough hike. I needed to be in top hiking condition to tackle it. Then it occurred to me; I could get in shape for the JMT by hiking the Long Trail. At first glance it seemed like a nice little warm up hike. It doesn't climb anywhere near 5,000 feet, there are shelters on a regular basis and towns all over the place. It sounded like a fun, easy way to get into hiking condition for the tough JMT. I could do it right before I headed west.

Obviously, I knew nothing about the Long Trail. Once I started doing a little research, the dream of a nice easy hike began to evaporate. This trail is steep. Per some information posted on the old Interweb, the trail has an average elevation change of over 500 feet per mile, nearly a 10% grade. By contrast, the Colorado Trail through the Rocky Mountains has an elevation change of just over 360 feet per mile. Pictures posted on some websites showed scenes of the Long Trail (LT) where metal rungs were drilled into vertical rock. I saw one photo where a guy was carrying his dog up a ladder. This was a real dog too, not some pocket sized designer pooch. I have to say, I've never been on any other trail that was too steep for a dog to walk.

The trail is wet too. The Green Mountains certainly aren't the highest in the world, but they are high enough to affect the weather. That means, among other things, more rain. Precipitation averages over seven inches most months, including August. That could make for my two least favorite aspects of backpacking: wet feet and mosquitoes.

Hmmm, if I skipped the Long Trail, just doing a junior doubleheader of hiking didn't sound quite as fulfilling as the Triple Crown. No, I was going to have to thru-hike all three trails. At the time, despite my research, I still didn't believe it could be all that difficult. I wasn't going to let facts get in the way of my opinion, or my plan.

I did learn enough to know the Long Trail would be an interesting challenge. The trail itself runs 273 miles along the spine of the Green Mountains of Vermont, traversing the entire length of the state from Massachusetts to Canada. It is the oldest long distance trail in the United States. The notion of the trail was conceived by James Taylor while at Stratton Mountain, one of the tallest peaks in Southern Vermont. The Green Mountain Club (GMC) was founded to support the concept and trail construction began in 1910. This was 11 years before the idea of the Appalachian Trail was proposed. Interestingly enough, the idea for the AT was first envisioned by Benton MacKaye while he was also on Stratton Mountain.

View from Stratton Mountain

By 1920 the Long Trail was over 200 miles long and by 1930 it had reached its present endpoints. To this day the GMC is the lead organization maintaining and managing the trail. They also publish a <u>Long Trail Guide</u>, the <u>End to Enders Guide</u> and a comprehensive map of the trail.

Beyond its age and steepness at times, the LT has a few other unusual attributes. There are over 50 shelters/lodges along the trail. Each is either a 3 or 4 sided shelter with both a water supply and latrine nearby. While carrying a tent or other shelter is necessary in case a shelter is full, most nights on the trail can be spent under roof. Some of the more popular camp areas have a GMC provided caretaker stationed to maintain the facility. Those spots often have a $5 per night camping fee. Otherwise there is no (monetary) cost to hike the Long Trail. No permits are required either.

The famous "Vermud" on the trail is also real. Long stretches of the trail have been improved with the use of puncheon, heavy timber set above the mess. However, despite this and other major efforts by the GMC, there are still more than a few spots where there is no option but to walk through mud and muck. I'd just bring extra socks. I was going on a thru-hike and it was time to start gathering my supplies.

Chapter 18: Quick Prep for the Long Trail

With the difficult climbs I'd be encountering on the Long Trail, I figured it'd be a good idea to try and lighten the load I'd carry compared to what I brought on the Colorado Trail. At that time, I felt I was reasonably lightweight while using major manufacturer products such as an Osprey pack and a Big Agnes tent. Then, fully loaded with two liters of water and four days of food, the pack came in at right about 31 pounds.

Electronics is one area I had gone overboard on the CT and would be an easy place to start losing a little weight. A new iPhone could be used to take photos, as a book reader and a spot to write journal entries. Leaving the iPad Mini at home saved 14 ounces. With more resupply stops, the 4-ounce Solar battery charger could stay home too. Between the trail being marked pretty well and a Long Trail App on the phone, the 5-ounce GPS wouldn't need to be there either. So far so good. Nearly a pound and a half saved just in electronics.

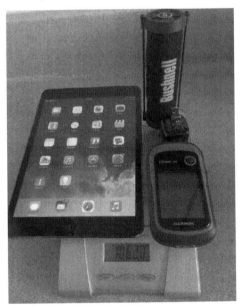

Banking on warm weather brought significant savings. There was no need to bring a cold weather jacket, hat or gloves. A summer weight sleeping bag saved some more. With the silk liner, a new 50 degree down bag was the plan to keep me toasty all the way down to 42 degrees. The savings of a pound only cost 25 degrees of comfort. (Actually, 15 degrees of comfort and 10 degrees of survival.)

The Long Trail has more opportunities for resupply, so three days of food would be the most I figured to carry, saving over a pound at my heaviest.

At that point, I was down to 26 pounds or so for a maximum weight. Unfortunately, there were add-ons to fight. The amount of food brought on previous trips was insufficient to say the least. Adding in more trail mix, peanut butter and soft tortillas put about a pound back. As an aside, I waited until the last minute to buy tortillas for my resupply boxes in an attempt to have them remain fresh on the trail. I needn't have worried. I don't know exactly what's in the Old El Paso brand, but they have a shelf life comparable to motor oil.

I also had to fight weight with the guides. The information needed on the trail was spread between a map and two separate guides. While they are all great sources of information, not all of it is needed while on the trail. Fortunately, a razor knife could be used to edit the books. Between the two, close to 100 pages were carved out of the final product. What was left was split in two with the second half being mailed in a resupply box.

All in all, there was still a weight savings of over 10 percent of the load I was used to carrying. Time would tell if it would be enough.

Never having hiked on the Long Trail, or anywhere in Vermont for that matter, one of my big concerns was footwear. What level of traction would I need? Should the shoes be waterproof? This was on top of my everyday shoe issues concerning Plantar Fasciitis in my right foot and a failed surgery on my left. Getting the correct shoe can be tough for me. By the way, if you ever have a Doctor tell you have a neuroma in your foot that needs to be surgically removed, consider a second opinion.

Anyhow, I was looking at a couple of trail runner options. They were Saucony Xodus, which I was pretty happy with while hiking the Colorado Trail, and Brooks Cascadia. My dilemma was as follows: the Xodus better protects my feet and has a very aggressive tread for great traction in gravel, mud and the like. However, the hard rubber sole doesn't grip smooth rock at all. Cascadia's softer, less aggressive sole is tougher on my feet, has less grip in most situations, but does significantly better when hiking on smooth rock. Which way to go?

An interesting service provided by the Green Mountain Club is a mentor program where you can connect with successful thru-hikers for advice. So, I put out my shoe questions hoping for input. What I got was a ton of information, occasionally contradictory, but helpful nonetheless concerning shoes and many other aspects of the trail.

The first opinion I received was to go with the Xodus as I needn't be concerned about smooth rock on the trail. The 2nd was that the Cascadia was the way to go. The tiebreaker was a hiker whose buddy had slipped and broken some ribs on the trail while wearing the Cascadia. Xodus it would be.

The Xodus comes in both waterproof and "regular" models and I received strong opinions on both sides of that issue as well. Eventually though, hearing a few times that, "Your shoes will get wet no matter what and if they're waterproof, they'll never dry out" sold me on the standard issue model.

Beyond that, there was the usual preparation of gathering equipment and food, compiling a tentative schedule and mailing resupply packages. This was a little different as I was also planning for my JMT hike at the same time. My turnaround was going to be quick and it was making me a bit nervous.

Chapter 19: Back on a Trail

With about a month before my planned departure for the John Muir Trail, I finished arrangements to hike the Long Trail and headed for Vermont. After a drive of just under 12 hours, I pulled into the Villager Motel in Williamstown, Mass. It was a clean, older place that was only $60 a night. The real bonus was the owner let me leave the truck there for the duration of my hike, though I'm not sure he realized how long I'd be gone. Between the local pizza place and beer cave, my evening was set.

The Long Trail could be accessed from The Pine Cobble Trail which began about three miles from the hotel. Since I didn't drive 12 hours to road walk, I made arrangements for a cab to pick me up at 7:30 the next morning and tried to get some slightly alcohol induced sleep.

The trail's first miles are a good indicator if you are in shape for the hike. Pine Cobble climbs around 1,500 feet in the first mile and a half. The path then takes you through a rock garden before meeting up with the Appalachian Trail (AT). It was a sunny, warm day and I was dripping with sweat by the time I finished getting through Pine Cobble and to the AT. Despite the warmth there was no humidity. Sections in the shade or in a breeze were very comfortable despite a forecasted high of 90 in Williamstown.

First view on Pine Cobble Trail

Once past the rocky first climb, the trail was very reminiscent of the AT, which shouldn't have been surprising as it also served as the AT. Several people were on the trail including Dave and Paul, two guys in their twenties from the Detroit area. They were also doing the Long Trail, but shooting to finish a few days quicker than I was. That seemed doable as their hiking pace was noticeably quicker than mine. At about 3 ½ miles in, I took an early lunch at the Vermont border, the official start of the Long Trail (LT). There were 273 miles to go.

The first miles of the LT consisted of pleasant walking through rolling woods. Overall, the trail surface was rockier than other trails I'd hiked, but not bad. I arrived at the Congdon Shelter (10 miles into the LT) about 3:30, right before a significant thunderstorm hit. Between the rain and not wanting to overdo it on the first day, I decided to stop for the night. The accommodations consisted of two double bunks separated by a table. I was the ninth person to show up at the (eight person) shelter.

This portion of the Long Trail was a lot busier than I was used to. Besides myself, Dave and Paul, there were a couple of AT southbound thru-hikers

(SOBOs) and four northbound thru-hikers (NOBOs). As the rainy evening progressed, more kept coming, setting up tents and looking for spots in the shelter to hang wet clothes and equipment. The final count was 8 tents nearby while it rained on and off till 5 am.

Since there was no more "bed" space, I set up on the table, which actually seemed roomy compared to sharing a bunk with someone I'd just met. The 10th, 11th and 12th persons in the shelter had less optimal accommodations. They were on the floor, surrounded by wet equipment and getting more than a little damp as the ongoing rain splashed into the front of the three-sided shelter.

Joshua was the 11th guy in the shelter. He was about 22 years old and was on his first ever backpacking trip. Laying on floor and not completely out of the rain, he was talking to anyone that would listen. "I love it outdoors! Everything is so green! I don't have allergies! This is so wonderful!"

Joshua was pretty entertaining to listen to. To him, hiking on the Appalachian Trail, which shares 100 miles with the Long Trail, was all rainbows and unicorns.

Things seemed pretty crowded to me, though it could certainly could have been worse. One NOBO told me that the first night he started in Georgia, not only was the shelter overly full, there were 40 tents set up in the area. Eventually that much crowding results in conflicts and there were a few tense moments on my first night in Vermont. One guy showed up late (9:30, after "Hiker Midnight") in the rain and inserted himself as the 12th person in the shelter. His headlamp appeared like a light show as he settled in and made himself some dinner. Eventually one of the SOBOs told him to knock it off. The newest arrival replied by thanking him for being so welcoming in the spirit of AT. That's when the name calling began. No blows were exchanged, but it was not pleasant. Despite that, I did sleep well on the shelter's picnic table, thanks in large part to earplugs. On the plus side, mosquitos were pleasantly absent.

In the morning, despite a couple self-serving apologies, the shelter atmosphere was still tense. I packed up quickly, hitting the trail at 7 am. Both the trail and vegetation were wet from the rain, but not too sloppy. There were a few skeeters moving but not enough to be a problem. The morning sun and breeze soon took care of that and the weather promised a good day. I was soon passed by Paul and Dave.

The 1,000 foot drop onto the road crossing at Rt. 9 was still a bit wet and extremely steep. It was obvious there has been a tremendous amount of work to arrange boulders into quasi steps but the stretch is still very slow going. Thankfully the north side had more switchbacks and less of a rock climb.

After that, the trail smoothed out and I started making good time through the heat of the day. At one point I caught up to Dave and Paul at a water stop, but they pulled on ahead. Everything felt good when I got to Goddard Shelter at 3:30 and decided to press on to Kid Gore Shelter for an 18.5 mile day. It was pushing 6 pm when I arrived. Dave and Paul were there, the shelter was already full, but they said I could sleep on the table again. The table had a 10% or so lean to it, and I passed. It was a nice evening so I opted to tent.

There was a tremendous view from both the shelter and my tent site and sunrise promised to be a good one. In addition, the group seemed much friendlier and upbeat than the crew the night before.

Most of the folks in the shelter were section hikers, including Beth from Connecticut. She was about 20 and on her first solo camping trip. She had a Sawyer Squeeze water filter, like mine, and her squeeze bottle had broken. Her duct tape repair wasn't cutting it, so I lent her mine. Despite her equipment problems she was having a great time.

Dave and Paul had already realized that they brought way too much food. They had gallon Ziploc bags of both oatmeal and instant potatoes that they were trying to give away. I passed on the offer as it was only about ten miles to Stratton Mountain Ski Resort. I was counting on a resupply box, room, and a restaurant waiting for me there. The evening was nearly perfect, dry and warm; again no mosquitos. It was starting to look like my August start was all the bug repellent I would need.

Kid Gore Shelter sunrise

After breakfast at the shelter while watching a perfect sunrise, I headed out. The trail began with a rugged 500 foot climb that had me moving slowly. Once the climb was complete, the trail surface improved, and I was able to make some good time. Nearing the base of Stratton Mountain, I met a NOBO AT thru-hiker, Sunshine, and we walked into some great trail magic. Roy was assisting his wife, Jersey Girl, hike the AT, but also providing treats for other hikers as well. He'd set up in a parking lot with a stove and was making sausage and egg sandwiches. Also on the menu were OJ, milk, doughnuts and Kit Kat bars. I did not pass on the chance at a second breakfast.

I don't typically provide unsolicited trail advice, but I did tell Sunshine she might want to set her pace to match Jersey Girl. If she could keep running into Roy, she might not have to pack near as much food.

The climb up Stratton Mountain was steep to start, then leveled out giving the false hope that you had topped out. Then it got steep again. On the way, I ran into and thanked Jersey Girl for her generous husband. At 40 miles into the LT and just over 3,900 feet, the peak of Stratton Mountain is the tallest point on the first half of the trail. The views from the fire tower were tremendous. It's no wonder this was the spot where the ideas for both the LT and AT were conceived.

Stratton Mountain Fire Tower

From the mountaintop, it was easy to spot the resort where my resupply waited. Though standing right underneath a cell tower, I could not make a connection. After getting part way down a ski run, I was finally able to get through and they said to just keep walking. I did have my first fall of the trip on the slick grass of a black diamond ski run, but was unhurt. I strolled into the Stratton Mountain Ski Resort at mid-afternoon.

Chapter 20: Stratton Mountain Mystery

The resort had a very nice room waiting for me, but the desk staff could not locate my food package. Per the Post Office tracking number, it had been delivered three days before, but was nowhere to be found. They sent out an email throughout the resort as a package APB. They also suggested I call the Post Office in the morning in case their mail carrier had somehow taken it back.

In a worst case scenario, there was a convenience store on the property where I could resupply in the morning and the ski patrol stated they would haul me back up the mountain to continue my journey. Being able to do laundry and take a shower made a heck of a difference, though my feet were sore from all the rock walking. Since it was the off season, the resort was somewhat deserted, but one bar was open and it was $2 taco night. I started with two, got two more, then three more, then a salad for dessert. Being warm and clean with a full stomach and a cold beer just made the world a better place.

In the morning, the Post Office said they had indeed delivered the package and mentioned this wasn't the first time the resort had lost a box. I checked with several personnel and they were unable to find it. With no better option, I dropped $72 at the convenience store. I wasn't looking forward to eating microwave Mac n Cheese with no access to a microwave.

Once the new resupply was packed up I met with Charlie of the ski patrol and he hauled me back up the mountain on an ATV. Charlie was a very nice guy and asked about my stay. I told him everything was great, except of course the package issue. He got me back to the LT at 11 AM. A late start to be sure, but there was a lot of downhill and I made good time. I even covered one 3.6 mile stretch in an hour. The plan was to make it to Bromley Mountain. There were some great areas to camp near Stratton Pond, but I forced myself to press on. The trail was a bit mucky in spots, though work had been done to alleviate that issue.

By 6 PM I'd finished 16 miles and strolled into Bromley Shelter. It was close to full, but wooden tent platforms were also available. Since the sky remained clear, I took the last of four platforms.

While setting up I checked my phone and noticed a voicemail. It was from Stratton Mountain Resort, stating they had my resupply package ready to be picked up. It had been at the ski patrol the whole time. As I wasn't about to walk 16 miles the wrong way, I asked them to just mark it "return to sender" and give it back to the Post Office. Dinner was the first of a few packs of microwave Mac n Cheese. I just added hot water and treated it like a freeze-dried dinner. Don't do that. After a ten minute wait I ate some hard macaroni swimming in cheese drink. The mental note was: next time cook it for a while.

The water supply was a small spring about a quarter mile downhill from the shelter. There I once again ran into Beth from Connecticut. (I had lent her a squeeze bottle back at Kid Gore Shelter so she could filter water.) Since then, she had been given a bottle by another hiker. Her hike was ending the next day, but she was thrilled with the experience. "I love it that the trail is so social. Even though I'm hiking alone, I never felt like I was ever really alone."

I had been feeling pretty good about my speed that day until I got in the tent and my bedtime reading was the book about Jennifer Pharr Davis's record setting hike of the AT. Over the entire trail she averaged close to the pace of my best downhill mile.

Through the night the temperature dropped to 45 degrees. The fifty-degree bag and liner seemed to be enough. That was a good thing since my extra clothes were in the elusive resupply box.

Chapter 21: Getting into a Rhythm

One noticeable difference between the Long Trail and other long trails I've hiked is the abundance of latrines along the way. Every shelter or camping area had one. The quality of these varied quite a bit and the one at Bromley Mountain was, relatively speaking, fit for a king. Like many, it was a composting toilet and, unlike some, was clean, roomy and odor free. After your "transaction," tossing a handful of the provided wood chips in with your "deposit" kept things that way. The latrines had been quite an upgrade from digging a cat hole.

Once I was moving, there were some tough climbs in the morning. Two of the most challenging were Bromley Mountain then Styles Peak. Both were short and steep climbs with a few handholds needed. The views were tremendous and worth the effort.

Two hikers head north off Bromley Mountain

Lunch was on Styles Peak where I ate with Beth. Singing Tom, an AT thru-hiker, also joined us. He started in Georgia on April 9 and the night of his first stop, the shelter was full and he counted 50 other tents. Much of the crowd had thinned by Neels Gap, thirty miles in. His favorite place was the Grayson Highlands (I really need to see them). His experience was that Vermont had better views than most of the rest of the AT, but had been relatively crowded with SOBOs and LT hikers adding to the numbers in the area. His equipment was holding up well. Interestingly, the one issue he had was with his Sawyer Squeeze water filter (same type that Beth had broken the bottle). His problem was a bit different though. At one point, it had suddenly clogged and all he could squeeze through was a bit of what looked like slime. After repeated attempts to back flush the filter, eventually a slug squirted out. I made a mental note to keep my filter in a Ziploc bag whenever it wasn't being used.

The highlight of the day had to be Baker Peak. It was not difficult at all until near the summit. That's when the trail became just a series of blazes painted on a rocky outcrop. Too steep for the trekking poles, I just grabbed rock with my hands as I climbed the last 200 feet or so. There's a bad weather (or strong sense of survival) bypass. The view was worth the climb though.

Climb up Baker Peak

By the end of the day I was running out of gas, probably somewhat from the previous day's 16-mile trek in seven hours. The last two miles was a slog along a creek to gorgeous Little Rock Pond. This one had a $5 fee for the shelter or to tent. The weather continued to look good so I opted to tent. Inside the shelter were three guys my age/older and I suspected the snoring might get loud. My hike for the day had gone from 7:30 to 5 to cover just under 18 miles. I was already looking forward to a break from convenience store food with a resupply from home and a room at the *Inn on the Long Trail* in a couple days. Though I tried to make a reservation, there was no cell signal to be had. That actually worked out to my benefit as the Inn had a discount for walk in hikers.

Little Rock Pond

Day 6 (7:00-6:30) started out like the last few, sunny and around 50. Highs had been near 80. Another rough climb started the day and then the trail passed through a couple of unusual cairn villages. There had been very few cairns along the trail, but these spots had hundreds. A bit spooky, like a Stephen King novel, Children of the Cairns.

After some great views, there was a long, steep drop. At this point, my attitude changed in a minute. On the downslope, I had my head down, watching the trail. For a while I could hear a stream and people below me, but that faded away. When the trail began to level out I looked up and "what the…" I was looking at a blue blaze, rather than the white blazes of the LT. Talk about taking the wind out of your sails. I was close to a parking lot, so went on down for an early lunch and to figure out what I had done wrong. After a quick study of the map, I decided my location was the White Rocks picnic area. I had missed a turn a half mile back up the hill which was actually marked pretty well. I hate walking the wrong way.

After getting back on track, the trail cut through a parking area at the base of Bear Mountain. The Green Mountain Club was there with 5 volunteers for "trail magic day." They had just finished laying out a spread including watermelon, cookies, lemonade, hot dogs and some doughnuts. If I hadn't missed that turn, I may have missed an unexpected feast. Eating and visiting with those fine folks put me even farther behind my daily goal, but it was well worth it. That meal supplemented my convenience store resupply and the extra calories helped power me over Bear Mountain which, though not overly tall, was indeed a bear.

From the peak of the mountain, the trail traveled mostly downhill for over four miles; till the bottom of Clarendon Gorge. After crossing the Mill River on a suspension bridge there were two brutal climbs out of the Gorge. First was a rock scramble climbing around 600 feet in a half mile. The second was just straight up dirt trail. Things moderated after that and I was able to pick up the pace. At one of the more level spots I passed an old rock wall. Apparently the area had once been plowed farmland.

I was very happy to see Governor Clement Shelter, the end of the day's 19 ½ mile walk. It was a long one. I spent a little time talking with Peter the caretaker along with his parents and siblings who were there to visit. The shelter was an old stone one, built in 1929 and fairly gloomy. Since there were already several folks inside, I once again set up my tent nearby at one of several nice spots. Water was handy with a beautiful stream close enough to lull me to sleep.

After a good night's rest, I ate breakfast with a couple guys in their 50's. They were test hiking to decide if they could handle the AT. They had hiked most of the LT before and said I'd love the northern section other than a few specific climbs. We talked a bit about gear and they were entranced by my $8 canister stove with an igniter. After eating I packed up quickly and was walking by 7 am. Based on the map the morning looked to be a rough one. The trail climbed 2,400 feet in just over four miles to top out near Killington Peak. The grade up the mountain turned out to be very smooth dirt and easy on the feet. That was a good thing as they were sore from high miles on rocky trail. The area was also toad central and they were acting as if they owned the trail. None hopped out of my way. At most they took a step or two to the side.

The climb up Killington was tough but doable as the trail wound up the mountain. There were just a couple short scrambles over boulders. After passing the trail to Shrewsberry Peak, the trail got nice and smooth, even somewhat flat the rest of the way to the high point. After a few photos of the view, it was time to start dropping in elevation again.

If any purists are still reading this, prepare to be upset. I was soon once again following blue blazes, but this time on purpose. The Shelburne Pass Trail was the historic LT and AT up until 1999 and a more direct path to the *Inn on the Long Trail* than the new route. Following the official LT to the Inn (and my next resupply box) would have been longer, and involve a mile of road walking. My thought at the time was, "That ain't happening." Since I'm an old guy, it seemed fair to walk the old route. (Hike Your Own Hike.)

Inn on the Long Trail

I arrived at the Inn at about 12:30 after a ten-mile day. I had passed the 100-mile point of the hike! My resupply box was actually there! Happy day! No more microwave food cooked without a microwave. The Inn is a neat, rustic old place and I got a room for the night. With the early arrival I had plenty of time to clean up, do laundry and arrange my new supplies. An Irish pub on site had Guinness stew, giant burgers and cold beer. I was set for a productive afternoon.

Chapter 22: Goodbye to the AT

My schedule had me taking the next day off. My feet said stay with the schedule, but the weather said go. The decision was put off until the morning. When I dropped off a couple extra items into the hiker box, I noticed some big bags of oatmeal and instant potatoes. They looked like the food Dave and Paul had tried to palm off on me way back on my 2nd night on the trail. Those two had also resupplied at the Inn and must have decided to lighten the food load right away.

Breakfast was included with the room and I got an omelet, sausage, hash browns, toast and OJ; enough to hold me for a couple hours. The weather called for a beautiful day followed by days of rain. It would be tough to leave a nice Inn and walk out into miserable weather. The decision was made: skip the zero day and head out while the getting was good. I hit the trail about 8 am.

From the Inn, the most direct route is to continue on the Sherburne Pass Trail for just a short distance until hitting the AT. From that point, I followed the AT south for about a mile to where the AT and LT split. From there, it's northbound on the Long Trail again, but the path is no longer shared with the AT. For the next several miles the LT had a nice dirt tread. Less wear and tear exposing the rocks and roots? There were definitely less hikers on the trail through the day.

The trail had no big climbs or drops on that section, but it was a tough day. That may have been because I was scheduled for a zero day. Weather was sunny and cool, but the trail was a tunnel of green with no big views.

I arrived at Sunrise Shelter at about 6:30, completing a 19+ mile day. The shelter was empty when I arrived. Steam from England, Ben from Belgium and couple from California all rolled in a little later. Steam had walked 19 like I did, the others 14, but all agreed it was a difficult day.

It was sprinkling in the morning but I got moving early and was the first out of the shelter at 7 am. That was a mistake. Rain and wind picked up as I climbed the aptly named Mount Horrid.

From there I dropped into Romance Gap, though with the degrading weather felt more like Nasty Break-up Gap. Dirt on the trail had turned into the famous "Vermud."

Rocks and roots got slick and the going was slow. I arrived at Sucker Brook Shelter by 11. It seemed perfect for a long lunch while watching the rain and deciding what to do. The next shelter was nearly ten miles. By noon, it was painfully obvious the rain wasn't going to quit. The only thing worse than hiking in the storm would have been sitting in the dark, leaky shelter watching the storm. So, I headed back out into it.

Vermud

The miles went by slow as the trail transformed into a creek and occasionally a pond. There was a very tough climb out of Middlebury Gap, but the rain finally slowed to just drizzle and fog. By late afternoon the rain had stopped. My day ended at Skyline Lodge after about 16 miles. Because lodges have four walls instead of the shelter's usual three, I could get dry and warm, but my shoes and hiking clothes were soaked. There was no need to work to dry them out as more rain was predicted.

A fellow hiker in the rain

I had arrived at the lodge at about 6:30. A couple was already there section hiking. It's easy to tell the thru-hikers from the shorter haul hikers based on the food brought along. They had beer, pizza and created a seven step homemade soup. I had a freeze dried Mexican fiesta. Steam rolled in about 7:30. He had a tough day. I know that because he said "tough day." That was all he said as he ate dinner and immediately went to sleep. He still hadn't moved when I left at 7:00 the next morning.

It had poured overnight with a drizzle continuing through the morning. I fell once on slick rock and the mud was a quagmire. At one spot was an intersection with no markings. I started down what I figured was main trail, but there were no blazes. I began getting worried as the trail continued steeply downhill, still with no blazes. Finally I remembered Guthook, a Long Trail GPS map App I had downloaded to my phone before the trip. Guthook had me located on the trail, which was a big relief.

By afternoon the sky had cleared off and everything improved. Rocks were drying up and getting stickier. Mud was still there, but it only took token efforts to miss the worst of it. I did fall on the way downhill to Lincoln Gap. Wet or dry, the slick rock slabs were tough to navigate.

After crossing Lincoln Gap, the trail started up the steep incline of Mt Abraham. About halfway up the mountain I stopped at Battell Shelter for a 16 mile day. The area ended up crowded with six (including me) in the small shelter and another eight or so in tents. One hiker, White Flower, spent quite a bit of time complaining about the lack of blazes on one section of the trail. I think I know where she meant. Steam rolled in around 7 and I heard the same complaint again.

It was a very nice group though. Jen walked in late planning to just hike up Mt Abe in the morning and then back down. Her supplies consisted of a big deli sandwich, some water and a bottle of bourbon. She generously offered me some of the adult beverage as "nobody should have to camp without bourbon."

There was also a family tenting as a final getaway before their daughter moved to Denver. We talked a bit about the Colorado Trail and they offered me some extra jerky they had. I gratefully ate it as I was losing weight and low on food. The tough trail and weather conditions had me burning through massive amounts of calories. We had an interesting conversation about the daughter's plans for the future and even a little "meaning of life" type stuff.

Of course not everyone uses the trail for deep thinking. I asked Steam during dinner what he was going to do once this was over. He said he was going to wash his bowl and go to bed. I said I meant bigger picture. He said he hadn't thought beyond getting his bowl clean and going to sleep.

It turned out to be a cool and breezy night, testing the temperature limit of my bag. I was starting to realize just how difficult this trail could be. I was just over halfway (139 miles) into my journey.

Chapter 23: Conditions Degrade

Thankfully there was no rain in the morning, but in the thick fog everything was wet. There were some very tough rock scrambles over damp granite as Steam and I assaulted Mount Abraham. In a moment of deeper thinking, Steam mentioned that if it were easy, everyone would do it. We soon spotted Jen already heading back down. She said it was clear at the top and the view was great. I suspected a lie.

Steam rises into the fog

Once I made it to top with Steam, visibility was less than 100 feet and misty, like in a cloud. At other view spots during the morning the results were the same. As I was low on food, an early lunch was two tortillas and the end of my peanut butter. I mixed up a protein drink which totally emptied my food bag. When I'm on the trail, it can be a constant battle between having a light pack and enough food. Often as not, the light pack wins. Steam powered on as I ate. The trail was still very sloppy in spots from the recent rains.

When the trail started to drop, it was as steep in places as I'd seen. Several spots had metal rungs driven into the rock to use as a ladder. On some other slopes I wished for rungs as I lowered myself down using trees. As hungry and tired as I was, I started to worry about getting hurt.

Rungs for the trip down

Eventually I finished a 10 mile day at Appalachian Gap and started hitchhiking towards Waitsfield where I had a room reserved. The very first car that came by picked me up. The driver was with search and rescue in the Mt. Mansfield area. I hoped I didn't see him again.

I was dropped off at the door of the Hydeaway Inn where they gave me a Coke and some chips to hold me over to dinner. While I took a hot shower, the staff washed and folded my laundry and delivered my resupply box to the room. BBQ was the daily special and the sun broke out. Maybe the day wasn't so bad after all.

As soon as the restaurant opened at 4:30 I was there ordering the pulled pork sandwich and Cole slaw with fries. When 7:30 rolled around the order was for the salad and 2 hot dog meal, followed up with a bowl of chili and homemade cookies and ice cream for dessert. The room was very nice, in a little private hallway to a couple rooms. I wondered; is this section just for hikers? Considering how I smelled upon arrival it made sense. Even 2 showers couldn't get my feet clean from the Vermuck. A complete cleaning might involve a wire brush. Luckily I'm typically not a sandal guy.

After a great night's sleep, it was a late start back to the trail. Breakfast started at 8 and the first shuttle back to the trail was shortly thereafter. After spending the night on the air vent, my shoes were somewhat dry; a real plus. I did break down and go with shorts, ticks be damned. Frankly, the bugs on the trail had been surprisingly and pleasantly absent.

I shared the shuttle back up with Sprinkles and No Key who were also thru-hiking. They actually walked AT in 2012 and had hiked at times with Golden, who had hiked with me on the Colorado Trail. They loved the Long Trail though Sprinkles had been terrified on some of the slopes. She stated at one point that she thought the trail was trying to kill her.

After a very hilly morning we had lunch at Coles Cove Shelter. There was an ominous warning posted that the next stretch of four miles could take 4-5 hours and was extremely dangerous when wet. If we got through that section there was an additional warning about bear problems at the next shelter.

View from Burnt Rock Mountain

The climb up to Burnt Rock Mountain was indeed tough with a lot of exposed rock. Views were incredible but with storm clouds beginning to build in the distance, I wanted to get off the peak while the rocks were still dry. Dropping down was a challenge with multiple, slick drops. The highlight, or lowlight depending upon how you want to look at it, was Ladder Ravine. At one point I had to use a knotted rope to lower myself to a ladder bolted to the stone wall. Mount Ethan Allen was even higher, but less exposed both up and down. It was still a tough traverse, often needing trees along the trail to pull up or lower down. Overall, I fell three times through the day, once while hanging on a tree and tweaking my shoulder. Sprinkles fell and ripped her pants. Up to this point I hadn't realized backpacking could be an adrenaline sport.

Montclair Glen Lodge

After about 8 hours and only 11 miles, we called it a day at Montclair Glen Lodge, another four sided enclosed shelter. A caretaker, Melanie, was on site and emphasized no food could be in the lodge due to the problem bear in the area. Claw marks on the building reinforced her words. A heavy, metal box was chained to a tree outside and, though it had been flipped over by the bear, it was the spot to store food.

Sam from New Hampshire rolled in a little later. A self-professed "peak-bagger," he had climbed all 48 of the 4,000 foot peaks in his home state. He told me that he had been on some tough hikes in the White Mountains, but nothing like he just done. Sam seemed a bit grim as he said he had been "on his ass a dozen times" and the LT had "a lot of effort without much reward."

In the morning I would be climbing Camels Hump which is over 4,000 feet in elevation. This iconic mountain is the highest undeveloped peak in the state and an image of it was used for Vermont's quarter. Looking at the guide, the climb and descent appeared to be as steep, or possibly steeper, than anything to this point. As a thunderstorm passed through, removing any dry spots from the rocks, I spoke with Melanie about what to expect on the mountain. She stated that there was quite a bit of exposed rock on both the climb and descent. It was mostly Gneiss going up and Schist on north side. A quick geology lesson. Gneiss is considered to be a coarse grained metamorphic rock. In contrast, metamorphic Schist has sheet-like grains in a somewhat parallel orientation. In layman's terms, if you've been slipping on the Gneiss, the Schist will really hit the fan when you get to the descent. I got a poor night's sleep.

Chapter 24: From Bad to Worse

Camels Hump in the clouds

There was no rain in the morning, but the entire peak was hidden in clouds. There would be no views and the trail would be wet. The first mile and a half were tough, but doable with several hand over hand climbs. About a quarter mile from the summit there was an optional bad weather bypass trail around the peak. As I stood at the intersection studying my options on the map, No Key and Sprinkles showed up. No Key was bleeding and Sprinkles was adamant about taking the bypass. She talked No Key into it. Sam also arrived and went for the summit. At this point, we were in heavy fog and the rocks were wet. I decided that I was in "bad weather" and took the bypass. The trail dropped a little below the fog and there were some decent views I wouldn't have gotten from the top. Regardless, I fell twice even on bypass.

Once the bypass reunited with the LT, the trail began a precipitous drop into a world of Schist. I had started to think I was wearing the wrong shoes before, but at this point lost all semblance of traction. There were long stretches of wet sloped rock where I had trouble even standing, let alone walking.

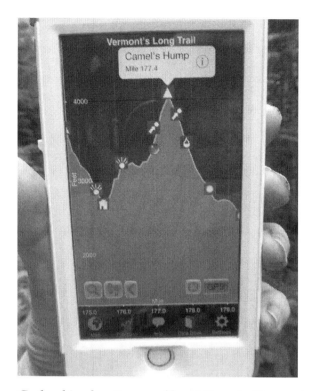

Guthook's elevation profile of Camels Hump. At times, it seemed that steep.

Working from tree to tree it took eight exhausting hours to cover the eight miles to the road crossing near Waterbury. It was very easy to picture myself alone on the trail with a broken femur. I ended up falling six times on the way down. There was no way I was going to get to my planned stop for the night; or any shelter for that matter. In addition, this meant I couldn't reach Stowe and my resupply on schedule and would run short on food. At that point it began raining again so the upcoming climbs would be treacherous as well. Things were looking bleak.

I needed more food. Contrary to my research, I needed different shoes. I needed a zero day and an overall slower schedule, but didn't have the time to spare. Like many, I had underestimated the difficulty of this trail. When I was younger, I probably would have pushed on despite the issues. However, as Muhammad Ali once said, "A man who views the world the same at fifty as he did at twenty has wasted thirty years of his life."

My initial thought had been that this hike would be a warm up for the John Muir Trail. Now it was looking like, if I finished, I'd have to rush out to California and start that trail exhausted and underweight. I decided not to push it. I'd head into town, find a way home and look to finish with different shoes when my schedule allowed.

As I stood in the parking lot attempting to reserve a room in Waterbury, a group of three Canadians finished their hike of the mountain. They spoke mostly French, but knew enough English to describe the trail with some colorful language. Of the many four letter words used, the term "easy" was not one of them. In addition, they offered me a beer and a ride to town. Things began to look up.

It was Friday night and both hotels in town were full, but I got the last camp spot at nearby Little River State Park. There I used Interweb to arrange Amtrak/Greyhound tickets to get back to the truck. Leaving the trail unfinished was disappointing as hell, but I felt fortunate not to have gotten hurt. I had fallen more in the previous couple days than in the ten years before that. It truly seemed stupid to push my luck on another wet mountain while running on little to no food. I didn't know how it would work out, but I knew I'd be back to finish the last 90 miles. It was a long drive home.

Chapter 25: Back to the Trail

Before I could consider returning to the Long Trail I had to get some hiking shoes better suited to stepping on piles of Schist and, oh yea, hike the John Muir Trail. While my existing trail runners scored high for traction in every review I found, I needed to find something significantly better before I could start planning my return. On the Vibram website I found a new (to me) option called "Megagrip." The site showed a backpacker hiking upside down. The ad bragged, "Megagrip: The new high performance rubber compound featuring unparalleled grip on wet and dry surfaces, rugged longevity and optimal ground adaptability." On the Merrill website I saw their Capra hiking shoe had the Megagrip sole as well as a "stabilizing hoof-shaped outsole." When was the last time you saw a mountain goat slip down a mountain? I bought a pair.

In the meantime, I had a date with the John Muir Trail and I wasn't going to waste that hard-to-get permit. A big part of the reason I had to leave the Long Trail was so I could get ready to hike the JMT. Well, instead of the LT serving as a training hike for the JMT, it had worn me out. Counterproductive to say the least. Now as the JMT is another story for later in the book, I'll leave it at this. I was able to complete it and if it's not already there, you should put that trail on your bucket list.

The Merrills didn't slip at all on the California rocks and the stiffer sole even helped protect my feet from getting quite as beaten up. I returned home near the end of September and spent a week trying to regain lost weight. Then I started watching the weather in Vermont. The hope was for a stretch of good days before the weather window closed for the season.

While I waited, I grew curious as to whether anyone had ever actually died climbing Camels Hump. However, when I searched the web for "Camels Hump Death" the top results were about a woman in Australia that had been humped to death by her pet camel. Apparently, it had been attempting to mount the family goat, but changed its object of desire. My search went "off track" after that and I never did find out if there had been any hiking fatalities on that particular mountain.

For several days things did not look good on the weather front. Hurricane

Joaquin was churning in the Caribbean. The Category 4 storm was the biggest seen in the Atlantic in years and some of the forecast models had it drenching the northeast. If that were to happen, my assumption was I'd need to give up on the idea of hiking the entire trail in one year; the basic definition of a thru-hike. All I could do was gather what food I would need, make a tentative plan of how to resupply without using the mail and watch the weather.

It wasn't until October 5 that it looked certain that the storm would stay far enough east to spare Vermont and the Long Trail. The forecast showed a few dry days in a row. While I was probably going to be flirting with winter weather before I could finish, I decided to take another shot. The next day I put my pack and a few bags of food in the truck and started driving towards Stowe, Vermont.

A couple last minute calls got me a reservation at the Arbor House which turned out to be a great choice. The owner, Michael, allowed me to leave my truck on site for a couple days. He also did his best to make sure I wouldn't be going hungry for a while. Breakfast was part of the room package; tasty and filling. When I turned down hash browns Michael told me I should eat them as I had a long hike ahead of me. He then handed me a fistful of energy bars to take along. As I was hiking "on the fly," I decided to use Stowe Cab for the shuttle back to the trail. The driver's wife happened to be a bakery owner so the fare included a bag of freshly baked cookies. Sufficient calories would not be an issue on this stretch. And so I was back on the Long Trail; hiking by about 9:30.

Winooski River

The trail had recently been rerouted in the area. After many years of effort, a trail specific bridge had been completed across the Winooski River, eliminating an extensive road walk. Once over the bridge, the new route was pretty smooth with, lo and behold, switchbacks. Not like the 100 off Mount Whitney, but not straight up either. After a few miles, the new route rejoined the old and the tread was back to its rocky, rooty self. The going was a bit slow, but my new shoes seem to grab better than the old ones. Vermont's fall colors were in full display, providing a beautiful diversion as I ground up Bolton Mountain. It was quite a climb, but my legs and lungs felt good, especially since I was carrying a light pack to help speed my progress. I was going stoveless on this stretch. My camp shoes and some small items were also left behind. In a last minute decision, I did put the tent back in the pack. I was concerned I might need it if I had some bad luck and couldn't make it to a shelter. Also, the pack looked empty and depressed without it.

It turned out to be a great day for hiking, cool and breezy all day with a bit of sun. Despite the light weight it took forever to peak out and the descent was steep including multiple ladders. I was feeling much more confident with the Megagrip shoes compared to my previous (lackadaisical grip) shoes, but the drop was still slow. No switchbacks, but many steps taller than my inseam. Despite the shoes holding on rocks, I did slip and fall on some mud, but no dramatic issues.

As I was moving along I noticed it was getting darker. It was 6 pm, the sun was setting and a map check showed I still had over ½ mile to go. Luckily, by that point the trail was pretty well off the cliffs and so I could pick up the pace. After some nervous hiking I arrived at Taylor Lodge with about five minutes of light to spare. Despite the darkening sky the view from the Lodge was outstanding. This would have been a rough place to hike by headlamp. The shorter amount of daylight would need to be a consideration from here on out.

After getting some water from a nearby stream in the dark, I ended up sharing the shelter with Maggie and Anna, two local section hikers on their last night of a five day trip covering 50 miles. Dinner was trail mix, summer sausage and a few ounces of cheese. It didn't seem like much of a reward for hiking 16 miles. I missed the stove already.

Chapter 26: New Highs and Lows

Being on east end of a time zone, Vermont still got light fairly early even in October. Just eating a couple breakfast bars sped the morning process and I was rolling soon after first light; around 7:30. There was a four mile climb up to the nose of Mount Mansfield; near the top was the "sketchiest" section of trail yet. More than once I looked at the trail in front of me and thought, "You have got to be kidding me." Luckily the weather was dry and sunny and my shoes were doing well.

Cars can drive to a spot nearly at the top of Mansfield so it was somewhat a shock to the system when suddenly there were dozens of people on the trail. Talking with Green Mountain Club staff at the Visitor Center I asked if the way down was as rough as the climb. One staff member suggested I take Profanity Trail. I dropped my pack at the intersection of that trail and headed up to the chin of Mansfield, the highest point in Vermont.

Day hikers heading up to the summit of Mount Mansfield

It was a great feeling to make it to the highest point on the trail. I felt like I was literary "on top of the world." With clear weather, the views were amazing. To the north, Jay Peak and even Mt Royal in Canada were visible. To west, Lake Champlain was obvious. Mt. Washington in New Hampshire was the highlight to the east. Another GMC staff member was stationed at the top greeting the many day hikers. He stated I was the first thru-hiker he'd seen in days and gave me a fortune cookie as trail magic. My fortune was to learn Chinese. That was a much better fortune than "You'll shatter your femur before nightfall" would have been.

View from the top

Profanity Trail was suitably named. I'm not sure how much worse the Long Trail could have been. It dropped straight down for a profanity filled half mile. I spent much of the time down climbing over nearly vertical boulders. After meeting back up with the Long Trail, I stopped for lunch at Taft Lodge. Once the leftover summer sausage and cheese were consumed there was another steep 2 miles out to Smuggler's Notch and Route 108.

The thumb was out for maybe 10 minutes before I got a ride back towards Stowe, the Arbor Inn and my truck. From there it was about an hour's drive to the Jay Peak (ski) Resort where a room was waiting. I had packed plenty of food in the truck to handle my resupply needs.

Working through the GMC I had made arrangements with Pat to pick me up at Jay Peak the next morning and drive me back toward Stowe where I had left off. Early that morning, I received a text from her stating that it was pouring rain and asking if I was sure about hiking that day. She was right about it pouring and the forecast was for continuing rain all day. Pat had a good point and was willing to drive me the next day. So, I headed down to the desk to rent my room for another night.

If I needed to take a zero day, Jay Peak Resort was the place to do it. Being the off season, there was no crowd and the rooms were reasonably priced. I had multiple restaurants to choose from including an "all you can eat" brunch. A convenience store carried snacks and there was even an indoor water park had I thought to bring a swim suit.

By evening, the forecast was looking pretty good. It called for dry weather the next three days, though colder. Beyond that however, the long range prediction was four days of rain, then two days of snow. My weather window was closing.

Pat was unable to give me a ride in the morning, but sent her husband Jim in her stead to drive me back to Smugglers Notch. He was a very nice guy and he and Pat have driven hikers around the trail for years. Unfortunately, the trail turned out to be significantly less pleasant than Jim. The path started straight up out of the notch and rain the day before had left everything wet and slick. The rain had come through with a cold front and there was a heavy frost at higher elevations. The going was slow, but I'd started at 9:30 and figured there was plenty of time to cover 11 miles before darkness fell.

After a mile climb, the trail leveled out, on the map. In reality the path was etched into the side of a steep mountainside and constantly climbed over boulders and tree roots.

Sterling Pond with frosty trees on the hill

After passing by the very pretty Sterling Pond, crowded with day hikers, I started climbing again through a ski resort. After a short climb on a ski run, the trail reentered the woods and there were several climbs where it was hand over hand grabbing roots to climb. After a bit it was back onto the ski trail. Apparently just walking the ski trail wasn't steep enough.

The down slopes were even tougher. While the shoes gave good traction uphill, they were no match for the steep downslope rock slabs, especially since they were wet and often covered with freshly fallen wet leaves. Nothing could get traction on the wet roots, which were frozen at higher elevations. I often had to just throw my trekking poles down a slope, turn around and climb down backwards. At times these slopes also multi-tasked as drainage swales so both hands and feet were soaked as I went.

In early afternoon, checking my progress, I realized I was going too slow to make the shelter I was shooting for. My other possibility was to stop early at Whiteface Shelter, 3,100 feet high on Whiteface Mountain. As cold as the day was, overnight there would be miserable. There was a good chance the wet trail would freeze by morning; trapping me up high for much of the day. To avoid that scenario, the only option was to go faster, pushing as hard as possible without endangering myself more than the trail already was.

On another steep upslope, I scrambled to the top of a big boulder pile, turned right and immediately had to drop back down through a mass of roots. As I looked for the best way down, I noticed an obvious way around the whole mess. It looked like the trail was routed purposely to make it even tougher than it needed to be.

That's when I lost it. I spent the next several minutes loudly cursing the trail designers and cursing myself for my decision to return. Why did I come back to this trail at all? Why come back when weather was forcing me to hurry, when conditions would be tougher and when I wouldn't have enough daylight to cover the needed miles?

Of course there was no answer from the trees, the rocks or the trail. Nature doesn't care if you're having a bad day or a tough time. It was all on me. After a bit, I knew I had to quit wasting time feeling defeated. There was no option but to hurry and hope I didn't get hurt. With that I put my head down and hiked. I'm sure there were several great views, but I didn't stop or even glance at them. No snacks, no water, just keep moving.

The slope off Whiteface was as steep as any, but I just grabbed trees and hoped my feet stayed underneath. Luckily I stayed upright and trail finally leveled out a bit the last two miles to the shelter. I arrived with 15 minutes of light to spare. My feet were hurting because, with leaves on ground, I couldn't avoid sharp rocks on the trail. I was dead tired and thinking tomorrow had to be a better day as I needed to do 16 miles.

Alone in the dark of Bear Hollow Shelter is not a great spot when you feel down and beaten. It was cold enough that I slept with my water filter to keep it from freezing. Before sleep took over I laid there thinking, "This trail may be scenic, but the views aren't worth the price of admission." Being 219 miles into the journey didn't matter at that point. All I wanted to do was to get back to my truck. It was actually a good thing it was parked 50 miles away, otherwise the hike would have been over right then and there. I had three more days of hiking to get back to civilization. Damn.

I'd say what a difference a good night sleep can make, but that was not the case on this day. I woke up around 6 with my head spinning. Dizziness had bothered me some before on trails, but this was worse. I almost fell down stepping out of the shelter. Despite the issue I decided to get an early start to make the most of available daylight. After a quick granola breakfast I was hiking with a headlamp by 7. The trail stayed smooth and fairly level in the river valley which was a good thing as moving my head made the dizziness worse.

Perhaps the smoothest trail of the trip

The balance problem had bothered me a bit on the JMT, but I had just assumed it was altitude. The issue had disappeared when I was at home or even staying in a hotel. What was I missing on the trail? Besides Bud Light of course.

I began to think, beer free hiking aside, that it might be dehydration so I forced down a couple extra liters of water through the day and the problem faded considerably. I would have to see what the next morning would bring.

Throughout the day the weather was cool, partly cloudy and dry. There was a bit of confusingly (to me) marked trail down towards the Lamoille River. I followed a road, a short section on a bike trail, a road crossing then dirt tread once again along the river. The guide mentioned a ladder down to the river channel, but it was missing (washed away?) and I strolled right by my turn. After losing the trail for a bit and a short backtrack I found the good sized bridge across.

Once I crossed the river, there was a subtle, but significant difference in the geography of the area. The mountain was not as steep as recent ones had been and it even held some topsoil. This meant the trail was mostly dirt rather than rock/roots. The recent rain had been absorbed and footing was dry and smoother. The trail was still steep in places. Gravity was still working the same, but everything was walkable. No climbing required. There were spots that even followed old Forest Service roads and climbed or dropped gradually. It began turning into a great day! The distance was adding up as I had traveled over seven miles by 10:30. Lunch was at the unusually designed Roundtop Shelter.

The trail also passed through a section of forest crisscrossed with plastic tubing. The plugged stiles in the big maple trees were already set to start producing that famous Vermont maple syrup come spring.

This stretch was definitely less steep. For the first time in a while, I passed an ancient looking rock wall in the forest. Many years ago this was plowed farmland.

View from Laraway Lookout

The climb up to Laraway Lookout was 1,400 feet over less than two miles, but again all walkable with no "climbing" needed. The view from Laraway was fantastic, but the map indicated a steep decline off the peak. There were no issues though as the steep slope was still holding soil and I cruised into Corliss Camp at about 4 pm. Corliss is a very snazzy cabin that I would have to myself. In fact, other than day hikers near road crossings, I had the entire trail pretty much to myself since Mount Mansfield.

Corliss Camp

I was trying Pack It Gourmet freeze dried food on this stretch and was pretty happy with the results. Hamburger tortillas were on tap for dinner, with an extra helping of water. As the sun set, the temperature began dropping. However, it remained warm enough that there was no need to cuddle with the water filter like the previous night.

There was even a strong cell signal there. Checking the weather, things looked good for one more day, then started degrading badly. My window of opportunity was beginning to close. Regardless, there was good sleep to be had as the enclosed shelter was quiet and dark.

I awoke in the morning to a shaky world. The dizziness was better than the day before, but a long way from cured. The hike up Butternut Mountain had some short climbs but nothing I couldn't handle despite my poor balance. Once again, the issue seemed to improve through the day. There was no view to be had on Butternut. Just a climb to the peak and then straight back down.

During the descent off the mountain, I stopped to filter water near Spruce Lodge. Strolling the other way was a backpacker; the first I had seen in a while. Jason was attempting a southbound thru-hike. Discussing trail conditions he warned me about significant muck past Mt. Belvedere. I wished him luck though I was thinking his weather window didn't look promising. It looked like it might be snowing in a few days and he still had the big mountains to get over.

After some ups and downs, the trail dropped into Devil's Gulch, a small, boulder strewn narrow canyon. It actually wasn't bad to pick through and was a pretty interesting spot.

From there though, I faced an approximately 2,000 foot climb to the top of Belvedere Mountain. My thighs began feeling really tired for first time since my return to the trail. The slope seemed to go on forever and then I just had to tack on a bit more distance to climb the fire tower at the peak. It was worth the effort since there was a clear sky and sweeping views of fall color.

Belvedere Mountain view

Jason was right though. Dropping off Belvedere, the muck returned with a vengeance. It was hard to believe there was so much standing water and slop a full three days after the last rain. What was that stretch like during wet weather? Despite my attempts to keep to the higher ground, muck topped my shoes on several occasions. There would be fresh socks in the morning, need them or not.

Don't slip off the logs

Tillotson Camp was a fully enclosed shelter that from the outside looked like a yard barn, but with an interesting drop down window that let in some light and a great view. Despite being pretty high up at 2,500+ feet, there was a nice brook nearby. I arrived there about 5:30 after a 15 mile day. The weather remained clear and warm through the evening. It had been warmer each night since needing to wear gloves and hat in the sleeping bag a couple nights before. Once again I had the place to myself. After the sun set, the wind picked up and howled all night. While this was partly due to the exposed location, I could also feel a change in the air.

In the morning I was greeted with continued dizziness. This was getting old. The wind continued blowing and low grey clouds were starting to blow in. I was hopeful the rain would hold off a while as I had 12 miles and five mountain peaks to cover before the trail returned me to Jay Peak.

Throughout the morning the rain threatened as I traveled up and down Tillotson Peak, Haystack Mountain, Bruce Peak, Buchanan Mountain and Gilpin Mountain; not to mention Domey's Dome.

In several spots it was back to pitching the hiking poles down the slope and down climbing the rocks. Despite the lowering clouds though, there were some nice views on some of the peaks. By early afternoon I was dropping down towards Jay Pass, Rt. 242 and a road walk back to Jay Peak Resort. I met an older man hiking up. He said he wanted to get in one last hike before the weather turned miserable.

I was still dry as I began the two mile road walk to the resort. There was little traffic so I didn't bother trying to hitch. With less than a mile to go it started to rain. With the resort in sight, one of the few cars on the road stopped and a former Long Trail thru-hiker asked if I needed a lift. Just as he asked, the rain picked up and I happily accepted a ride right to the door. The kindness of Vermonters near the trail was amazing. It was time for one last night at Jay Peak Resort. I was only about 12 miles from Canada.

Chapter 26: Oh, Canada

Unfortunately the weather forecast for the nearby town of Jay was rain for the next 3 days with lows around or below freezing; then snow. The mountains, specifically Jay Peak at over 3,800 feet, would be significantly colder and likely covered in ice. It was looking bleak. There would be no waiting this out. The weather window had closed.

I parked my truck along the side of the road and started hiking into the woods through a cold, driving rain. Jay Peak was completely enveloped in clouds. There would be no views. With my continued dizziness, the climb would be treacherous and I couldn't expect any other hikers to be around if I needed assistance. I already felt like I had pushed my luck more on this hike than any I'd ever taken and didn't see the point of pushing it any further. So what was I doing out in the storm? Hiking the Long Trail, of course.

While my minimal common sense dictated I not climb Jay Peak, the trail had another road crossing north of the mountain and that's where I was. Even if I couldn't walk every foot of the trail, I would walk as much as possible. And, unless I walked to the official "end" of the trail, I wouldn't feel like I had completed my standard of a "thru-hike."

The weather, if anything, worsened as I went. On the plus side, the trail was less extreme than recent miles had been. The stretch crossed just one peak. Carleton Mountain was a 500 foot climb and from there it was generally downhill the final mile and a half.

Canada

After a brief stop at the sign indicating the northern terminus of the trail, I went looking for the nearby monument indicating the Canadian Border. There was no Mountie there to take my picture. In fact, the high wind and horizontal rain made even a "selfie" out of the question. There was nothing to do but turn around and head back to the truck.

As I walked the undulating trail back, I thought about what a challenge this trail had been. Did I actually "beat" the Long Trail? Just as that thought crossed my mind, I slipped and fell one final time, sliding down a slope of wet leaves and schist. No, I thought. I did not beat anything. What I had done was survive the Long Trail.

I can say without reservation that the Long Trail was the toughest backpacking experience of my life. However, as time passes I become all the more glad that I did it. With every challenge in nature, there are rewards. By the end, the Long Trail provided more than its share of challenges, but also more than its share of rewards.

Part 4, Chapter 28: The John Muir Trail

When I arrived back home after failing to complete the Long Trail, I only had a couple weeks to recover and head west to the John Muir Trail. I had a permit to hike the JMT beginning on September 11, but it was from Tuolumne Meadows. This starting point was 23 trail miles from the actual start of the JMT at Happy Isles. Missing the first 10% of the 220 mile journey wasn't going to cut it as a thru-hike so I headed out a couple days early to cover all the mileage.

Preparations were a little hurried, but for the most part, complete. My equipment was together and the only resupply package had been sent by UPS. The logistics of getting back to the start from the end of the trail at Mount Whitney remained a bit iffy though. There are two different bus services that can be used in conjunction for the return, but as I was going very late in the season, they would not be convenient. One system was only running during the week. The other system only ran on weekends after Labor Day. Depending upon my finish day, there could be a long layover.

My pack, which I had lightened up while on the Long Trail, was going to be heavy again. A heavier sleeping bag, gloves, hat and a down vest added to the weight. I also needed to carry a bear resistant canister for the food. Even though I sprang for the expensive one, it still added a couple pounds to the pack. Carrying four days of food and two liters of water, I was going to put 34 pounds on my back. I didn't want to know what the pack would weigh when I left my resupply point with eight days' worth of food.

Between the need to rush, the permit hassles, ongoing fires near the trail, the heavy pack, the three day drive and paying $4 a gallon for California gas, I wondered if the trip was going to be worth the trouble. That concern evaporated as I drove up Tioga Road toward the east entrance of Yosemite National Park. The mountains and views were simply stunning. The giant slabs of rock are incredible and despite the drought, beautiful lakes and streams abounded. There were some wildfires in the area, but the air quality was holding up.

View from Tioga Road

Yosemite Valley was still pretty crowded despite it being after Labor Day. There were thousands of people near parking lots taking photos. I was struck by how many of the photo takers were not focusing on the scenery, but themselves. The grand cliffs served as little more than a new background for a collection of selfies. I just don't understand it. I doubt that the people I know would be enthralled by seeing countless shots of me blocking beautiful scenery. Even I wouldn't be interested in shots like that. I see myself in the mirror at least twice a day when I brush my teeth. That's typically enough. Perhaps the long drive just had me grumpy. I know I was looking forward to getting into the mountains.

On the drive through the park I checked in at the Wilderness Permit Office and mentioned that I planned to day hike from Tuolumne Meadows to the start of the trail in Yosemite Valley. In talking about available daylight, the Ranger suggested starting at Cathedral Lakes Trailhead so I'd only need to cover 21 miles or so. I could pick up the two miles from there to my permitted start later.

Tent Cabins

My accommodation was a tent "cabin" in Curry Village within Yosemite Valley. For $59, the cabin was complete with a queen bed, towels, a light and a bear resistant food box out front. All in all, pretty comfortable and the views of the surrounding peaks were amazing. Posted warnings about Plague carrying rodents were a bit disconcerting, but I never saw any mice. There were a couple restaurants and a convenience store within walking distance. It looked like I was set.

It was about 50 miles from my tent cabin in Curry Village to Tuolumne Meadows. The sun was just hinting at rising the next morning as I climbed into my truck and headed out. Arriving at the Cathedral Lakes Trailhead nearly 2 hours later I parked alongside the road. Everyone else was using windshield covers (to fool bears?) so I did too. My hike began about 8:30 at the Cathedral Lakes Trailhead. Starting with a consistent, though not steep ascent, the surface was a sand and dirt mix. In some spots it was almost like beach sand. One thing I noticed right away was the complete lack of blazes. Metal signs were at intersections, but that was it. However, the signage seemed to be plenty as the trail was very obvious. I was starting at 8,600 feet and felt a little short of breath due to the altitude. Just carrying a day pack there was no problem climbing though.

Cathedral Peak

Hiking through open woods, it didn't take long for the scenery to start getting spectacular. Heading toward Cathedral Peak the views just kept getting better. Near Cathedral Lake every direction was a postcard. Over five miles the trail climbed to 10,000 feet and the repetitively named Cathedral Pass. In this area were a couple high school aged guys that had begun hiking the JMT at Happy Isles. They looked pretty happy when I told them they were done climbing for a while. I continued on through another meadow with new gorgeous views.

The sun stayed strong and I took a break to put on sunblock. After a little over nine miles of hiking, the trail topped out again near 10,000 feet and started the long drop to Yosemite Valley. Trees around me started getting huge. A deer walked behind one and was completely hidden. A little while later a coyote strolled by, seemingly unconcerned with my presence. The downslope was steep, but a liberal use of switchbacks helped.

When I was almost exactly halfway on the day's hike I came across two couples taking a break. They asked if I knew how far it was to Tuolumne Meadows. Checking the GPS app on my phone (Guthook), I let them know they had 10 1/2 miles to Cathedral Peak Trailhead and that's the same distance they'd walked from Happy Isles. One member of the group told me that as the crow flies, they'd gone 8 miles and the standard trail multiplier was 1.5 so they'd gone 12 miles. I replied that as the crow walked, they'd gone 10.5. Once he pulled his map out, I politely taught him how to read it and how my walking crow was more accurate than his mathematically adjusted flying crow.

A short time later the trail passed through a burn area (fire in 2014) and dropped down through the desolation of charred standing tree trunks for about 2 miles. With the drought, nothing had even started growing back except right along a small creek. There were a couple tents set up near the creek. It seemed like an incredibly depressing place to camp.

Eventually I was back into a live forest and getting views of Half Dome. A large firefighting plane flew over towards an area of smoke. Once to the Half Dome Trail, I was joined by a parade of hikers. The steep switchbacks returned till I reached a flat stretch through Little Yosemite Valley. The trail crossed over the Merced River then circled back to get some great views of Nevada Falls.

Nevada Falls

There began an unrelenting 3 mile drop to the valley floor with the JMT chiseled into the wall of the valley. The trail surface eventually transitioned to asphalt as it headed steeply down, losing a final 2,000 feet in altitude. My knees and feet, already tired from the previous 18 miles, were complaining loudly about the pounding. However, it would have had to be much tougher going up with a full pack. I'm sure that tough start has ended more than a few JMT dreams. I silently thanked my bad luck in not being able to score a permit from the trail's official beginning.

It was about 6 pm when I reached Happy Isles and the end of the day's hike. In a lucky break, a shuttle bus pulled up just as I stepped off the trail. Grabbing the free transport, I walked within 10 feet of a deer that grazed unconcerned by the bus stop. And so I finished my first day's hike where many start, but had covered the miles nonetheless.

After another good night's sleep in the tent cabin, my task for the day was to pick up my wilderness permit and retrieve my vehicle. To get back to the truck, I could retrace my 21 mile hike of the day before or ride the free shuttle bus back to Tuolumne. The bus was pretty nice and even had plugs to charge my phone had I brought a cord. I was on the first bus of the day, leaving Curry Village at 7:45 am. Why didn't I take the bus yesterday you ask? If it were summer you'd have a point, but I really didn't want to finish the hike by headlamp and driving myself bought me more daylight. The bus didn't roll by my truck until nearly 10:30. I'd have been walking in the dark. Two more stops and I got off at the Wilderness Permit Station. There I picked up my permit for next day complete with the standard lecture about bear canisters, running off bears, picking campsites, soap, fires and packing out toilet paper. I was also presented with a "wag bag" in case I needed to poop on Mt Whitney. Although the bag didn't appear to require much of a learning curve, rest assured I intended to avoid that situation if at all possible.

Lunch was at the nearby Tuolumne Meadows Grill and then I enjoyed a leisurely stroll back to the truck. The trail was a bit confusing in the area, so be careful if you're a purist about walking the trail correctly. Of course, if you feel that way, you're probably not parked at Cathedral Lakes Trailhead. The drive back was interesting as a bear ran right in front of me. Back by Curry Village I spotted my first bobcat in "the wild" as it walked right past my tent cabin.

That's a lot of cat

Dinner in the village was a pizza and a beer. It tasted so good I had another pizza and more beer. The rest of the evening was spent getting everything ready and feeling like I might explode from all the food and drink. Out of an abundance of caution I kept the wag bag handy, but it was not required.

Chapter 29: Out of the Valley

Early the next morning I had a quick breakfast at the village's coffee shop, turned in my tent-cabin padlock key and drove back to Tuolumne Meadows. Luckily, I got the last spot at the Wilderness Permit Office parking lot. After double-checking that there were no bear attracting food wrappers left in the truck, I strapped the pack on and was walking by 9. My original schedule had me starting at the Cathedral Lakes trailhead, but the few miles I walked the day before put me farther down the trail. I'd have the choice of a ten-mile day or getting ahead of schedule right away.

Deer in a reflective mood along Lyell Fork

The section through the meadows and into Lyell Canyon was fairly flat and stayed near the absolutely gorgeous Lyell Fork. The stream was crystal clear and flowing nicely despite the drought. In talking with a few backpackers heading the other way, there would be plenty of water all the way up to Donahue Pass, though dry on the back side. The trail stayed flat for 8 miles or so and I made good time and felt good despite the full pack (34 pounds) on my back.

Once the climb began, I felt it immediately. Over the next two miles the trail climbed from 9,000 to 10,200 feet. The trail was well designed and climbed smoothly with switchbacks, but that didn't change the fact that I live at an elevation of about 800 feet.

The sun had been out through the day and the air was dry. At the Upper Lyell Base Camp I drained the last of the 2 liters I'd started with and started filtering some of the Lyell Fork water. Looking up ahead, I could see why the creek was running so well. There was still significant snow on the upper reaches of the mountains up ahead.

As I was bending over and straightening up to get water to filter, I got lightheaded. That settled it. It was only 3 pm, but after 10 miles I was done for the day.

As I scouted for a campsite, two bucks wandered thru the area, oblivious to my presence. All day, it seemed like deer were everywhere and completely unconcerned as I walked the trail near them. I found a great little spot among some pine trees that still had a nice view of the creek and the cliffs on 3 sides. Obviously, it was time for a nap.

My first camp. The black canister is the Bearikade

A couple guys from Fremont, CA showed up while I was asleep. One started fishing the small pond and immediately caught a nice brook trout that was to be their dinner. It would be the same dinner they had the night before. I could handle that kind of monotony.

Per my initial plan, there would be 18 miles to cover the next day. Fortunately, after another 1,000 feet climb over 2 miles to clear Donahue Pass, the rest appeared to be downhill or rolling. Hopefully it would be doable.

Near Donahue Pass

All my food was in the Bearikade (bear resistant container) set 200 feet or so away. There were a few non-food items that I kept in the tent, but I wasn't worried. I couldn't imagine a bear swinging by to eat my hand sanitizer when less than 100 yards away there were two guys awash in the smells of fried trout, trout breath and trout farts.

After a bear-free night I woke up a little after 6. It took about an hour to eat and break camp. The climb over the pass was significant, but not overly steep. The two miles to the pass were completed in about an hour. At the crest of the pass the JMT left Yosemite National Park and entered the Ansel Adams Wilderness area. The pass was followed by a long drop through a dry valley until I got below some more mountains with snow melt. So far there had been water pretty much everywhere. Even up on Island Pass the trail wove between ponds. Water levels were low, but the streams were still running.

More stupendous views greeted me near Thousand Island Lake with snow covered slopes above it. The water supply was refilled there and I followed the trail up and over a ridge. Eventually I started dropping back down and my heart sank. Was I walking back down to Thousand Island Lake? It sure looked like it. Same mountain in the background and the lake looked similar with some islands. As I walked, I tried to figure how I could have messed up so badly to be somehow walking in circles. As I dropped further down I finally realized that while the mountain was the same, the lake was not. I was at Garnet Lake.

Thousand Island; or possibly Garnet Lake

As I was walking I met two thru-hikers. One north-bounder just raved about the experience and the views I would be seeing. A bit later a southbound hiker caught up to me. The first thing Floridia said was he was probably quitting the trail once he reached Muir Trail Ranch. He told me the smoke from wildfires was bad farther south and he didn't want to walk in it.

I thought my day was about over when I left Shadow Lake heading for a campsite at Rosalie Lake. The two-mile hike to Rosalie was basically unrelenting switchbacks. Unfortunately, after that slog all the sites were filled with weekend hikers so it was on to Gladys Lake. I finally arrived there around 6 pm. All the sites were filled there too but Peter from NY offered to share his area. He was a nice guy, about my age and had been hiking the Sierras for 20 years. Though I hadn't planned on it, he talked me into stopping at Reds Meadow Resort in the morning.

I broke camp around 7:30. After a short climb it was all downhill to Reds. About halfway there, Peter caught up to me so I picked up the pace and walked with him. The trail to Reds can be poorly marked, so he guided me in through the Devils Postpile National Monument. The name comes from the pretty interesting volcanic formations.

We made great time to Reds, arriving about 10:30; just in time for a second breakfast and some ice cream. Peter was resupplying there and headed for the laundry/showers. Several other hikers were also there trying to decide whether or not to continue into the worsening smoke. After some more ice cream I headed out into the worst smoky haze of the trip. The hard climb out of Reds was partly through a burn area and the haze made it appear very fresh.

Apparently it wasn't all haze though as I began to hear thunder. Keeping up the strong pace from the morning I arrived at my planned destination (Deer Creek) for the day at 3. It seemed a little early to stop, but the next camp spot was another five miles. As I considered options, the rain started. I quickly put up the tent and dove in to ride out the storm. Decision made; hiking was done for the day. Of course it cleared off shortly thereafter. I was 67 miles deep into the trail.

Chapter 29: A Snowy Pass and an Empty Lake

While at Reds I saw a weather forecast showing continued thunderstorms. Because of that I wanted to get an early start and push hard to get over Silver Pass as early in the day as possible. Camping at over 9,000 feet though, it was a cold night. I put a hat on in the middle of the night to stay warm and brought in my water filter into the sleeping bag with me so it wouldn't freeze. Despite the cold I got up at 6 and was rolling by 7. Smoke was rather thick in the area so there wasn't much need to stop for pictures. I went into a forced march pace the first three miles - a relentless 1,000 foot climb. The trail bounced around 10,000 foot elevation the rest of the morning passing a couple beautiful lakes. The smoke/cloud cover thickened up, a cold wind began and for the first time of the trip I hiked with my rain jacket on. In late morning, after a big drop down to Fish Creek, I broke for lunch in a pine grove to help block the rain that was starting. By the time I'd finished eating, I needed the pack cover and rain pants too. Passing another hiker, she was stopped to dig out her gloves. I knew I'd have to empty my pack to get to mine or I'd have done the same.

The climb to Silver Pass was about 3 1/2 miles rising from 9,200 to nearly 11,000 ft. The steady cold rain and wind were not the most pleasant conditions. About halfway up the climb the rain luckily quit. Unluckily, it had turned into sleet and snow. The ice pellets were actually preferable to the rain and while the ground began to get covered, it never got deep enough to cause any problems.

Silver Pass

Once I thought I was close to the crest of the pass some hikers came the other way and one told me I was 5 minutes from the top. Enthusiasm renewed, I pressed on. When I hadn't reached the pass 20 minutes later, I was sorry for the encouragement. Finally topping out, all I wanted at that point was to get to a lower altitude and warm up a little. I kept walking at a brisk pace downhill through more snow which changed back into rain; finally slowing to a sprinkle. The drop was steep and few spots looked inviting to put up the tent. By the time I finally found one I had dropped 2,500 feet from the pass and covered over 20 miles for the day. At around 5:30 pm I set up right next to a big pine that would hopefully protect me from a huge widow maker (dead tree) that threatened the rest of the flat spots in the area.

At that point I was just a few miles from the cutoff trail to Vermillion Valley Resort. I had a room reserved for the next night and my resupply bucket was supposed to be waiting for me as well. Rain continued on and off through the night. I wanted to make the resort's 8:30 ferry across Lake

Edison so I planned to roll at first light, no breakfast. The plan was to get up at 5:30 or so. That was the same time the rain began to fall its hardest. I packed everything I could into the pack while still inside the tent. That worked fine until I had to put the soaking wet tent into the pack. I was glad to be heading to the resort. It would have been rough trying to dry everything out on the trail.

The lake is actually a hydroelectric reservoir and was low enough that the walk to the boat included a couple miles on the lake bottom. The boat ride in a cold, windy rain was shared with two other hikers: James and his son Thomas from England. They said they might drop out if the rain didn't clear the smoke.

View from the bottom of Lake Edison

We arrived at the resort just in time for an extraordinarily hearty and tasty breakfast. By the time I had showered and ran a load of laundry the sun was breaking out. The picnic table outside my room spent the sunny afternoon holding pieces of equipment to dry. With great food, a friendly atmosphere and a cold beer or two, Vermillion Valley Resort (VVR) was a perfect resupply stop.

I had originally planned on taking a zero day at VVR, but changed my mind. Arrival time that morning was about 10 o'clock having hiked 5 easy miles. That meant I had plenty of time to relax and get ready to head out again. All the usual resupply issues: food, laundry, clean up and high calorie meals were quickly taken care of. Plus, while VVR is nice, there was nothing much to do there. All power was from a generator that shut down at 9:30 pm and restarted at 7 am. There was no TV or phone service at any point, and Internet was $8 an hour. The lake was low enough that there was no water near the docks. Without any diversions, I was already missing the trail.

I did take considerable time refilling the bear canister. I had not sent any resupply package further down the trail to Muir Trail Ranch and so I would be leaving VVR with everything I needed to complete the trail. That included approximately 130 miles worth of food. (I figured on eight days.) I could carry my first day's food separately, but the rest needed to go into the Bearikade. Cramming 7 days of food into the 650 cubic inch canister was not easy. Eventually I made it happen though the odds of running low on calories were pretty good. As it was, I needed to stand on the lid to close it. My pack was going to be heavy.

Chapter 30: Heading out With a Heavy Load

In the morning, VVR staff took me, James and Thomas to the Bear Creek Cutoff Trail. We could have gone back the way we came in, but the staff recommended the Cutoff Trail, saying it was a beautiful hike. It's actually a bit longer than backtracking would have been and again, I'm not a purist.

Bear Creek

The route was definitely a gorgeous hike. The rain over the previous couple days had Bear Creek running strong with photo quality cascades and falls for miles. The climb out of Edison was steady, but not painfully steep. Overheating was not an issue as the sky was partly cloudy and temperature remained brisk. In addition, the rain had cleared to air of smoke; at least for the time being.

With the extra miles, I was thinking of ending the day at Marie Lake. It's a beautiful spot just short of the Selena Pass. Once I stopped walking though, the cold wind just ripped through me. Any spot flat enough for the tent was exposed. It was obviously going to be a cold night and a windswept lake near 11,000 feet was not the place to spend it. I did step off the trail to get some water. When I turned around, there was a coyote walking down the trail maybe 50 feet from me.

Marie Lake

Wind was just howling over the pass. I continued past Heart Lake as there was no cover there either, finally dropping down to Sallie Keyes Lakes around 10,000 feet. The drop was just enough to get out of the wind, with trees and the high wall of the pass for protection. It might have been the prettiest campsite I'd ever been on, up to that point.

Sallie Keys Lakes

The weather was clear and very cold overnight. I brought the water filter into my sleeping bag and kept it in my pocket through the morning. There was significant frost build up on the tent fly. I had cold granola for breakfast only because I wasn't sure the stove would work at that temperature. I got rolling about 7:30 with a long downhill stretch and passed by the Muir Trail Ranch cutoff well before noon. It seemed to have made sense not to resupply there so soon after VVR.

Leaving the John Muir Wilderness, Kings Canyon National Park was impressive from the beginning. The trail started up a massive gorge right on the edge of a drop to the San Joaquin River. There was a hand written sign warning of wildfires and smoke, suggesting that hikers should turn back. The smoke wasn't bad, so I pressed on. After a few miles the trail cut over to Evolution Creek, a stream that was dropping straight into the gorge with an impressive waterfall. The trail worked its way up a cliff and though the creek had settled down, I still had to switch to sandals when trail crossed it. This was the one spot on the trail that I had to wade. Once

I made it to McClure Meadow, I decided to stop even though it was only 4 o'clock. Besides still being tired from the previous day's mileage, the camp spot and views of the upcoming mountains were as pretty as it gets.

McClure Meadow camp view

In the morning I got rolling by about 7 am. The trail soon started the 9+ mile long climb to Muir Pass. I hiked with a few people through the morning including two older gentlemen. One was 75 years old and other 76. They had been doing the JMT for 13 straight years. The 76 year old's trail name was Tin Man because he had two titanium knees. They talked about walking slow, but it was still pretty impressive.

Overall the stretch was a hard climb but the views were outstanding. Beautiful lakes sat all along the way. At one point, the breeze had quit, no birds were in the area and there was no water running. Just absolute silence. So rare. Many people never know what complete silence is like. I made the 12,000-foot pass and only shelter on the trail about 1 pm. The shelter had tremendous views in all directions. It had been built, not for overnight accommodations, but protection from lightning and storms. No protection was needed that day as there was never a cloud in sky; just a bit of smoke. The trip down had lakes, streams and the stark beauty of the high mountains all along the route. I ended up camping in Grouse Meadow, 140 miles into the trail.

Near Muir Pass

Chapter 31: A Pass a Day

I was starting into a pattern. Climb to a pass in the morning, then head downhill as far as possible to set myself up for the next day's pass. In the morning it was 11 miles to the top of Mather Pass, a climb of 4,000 feet. The last 500 feet were in just a half mile through boulders. It was a very tough climb. Once at the top, I could see the campsite I had planned on was located in open rubble. On the way down I decided to keep walking as the lower I got, the better I felt. I ended up covering between 17-18 miles. As I was setting up camp Mike and Tao stopped by looking for a spot, so we shared. They were just doing a portion of the trail, leaving through Kearsarge Pass Trail. They told me rain was forecasted to hit in a few days. I had heard that before and didn't think much of it. Then they mentioned that rain could mean ice and snow on Whitney and the trail down was "gnarly." Their reasoning for leaving through Kearsarge Pass was they didn't want to take a chance on being snowed in between Forester Pass and Mount Whitney. I hadn't even considered that. Great. I could always use something new to worry about. As with the smoke issues, I decided to press on.

In the morning I got a 7 am start to climb up to Pinchot Pass. After a mile or so of downhill the climb began. This one was about 2,000 feet, much better than the last, but my legs were already tired from the big climb the day before. I topped out by 10:30 and the far side looked like a desert. The trail dropped 3,500 feet till the climb started for Glen Pass. There was a pretty interesting suspension bridge over Woods Creek at the bottom. It seemed like a good place to take a break with ample camping nearby. I was feeling a bit worn, but knew I should climb a bit to make the next day's climb a little shorter.

As I put on my pack, a woman crossed the bridge and started ahead of me. Eventually catching up, I asked the usual questions; when did you start (days after I did), how far you going today (30 miles). It turned out that Jen was an ultra-marathoner and shooting to hike the JMT in eight days. She had written for Trail Runner Magazine and knew many of the folks in the sport I'd only read about. Talking about the sport energized me and we took turns pacing up the climb towards Glen Pass. By 5:30 we had made it to Rae Lakes, several miles farther than I'd planned for the day. Jen had a snack, put on her headlamp and pushed on to clear Glen Pass three miles up the trail. She often ran through the night and hiking the pass after dark would be no big deal. I ended up with a 20 mile day and that was plenty for me. Rae Lakes was another incredibly beautiful place to camp. I also took the opportunity to take an extremely fast dip in the lake. If the water had been any colder, I think it would have been solid.

Rae Lakes

The day's hike started out of Rae Lakes about 7 with a beautiful sunrise. After walking for about five minutes a bear cub ran across the trail. Slowly walking forward I saw both the cub and mom sitting at a campsite by the trail. It looked like they were there for the day. I stood and talked to them for a while before they finally moved on and I could too.

Fellow campers

The climb up to Glen Pass had numerous false summits and took till 9:30. Met Evan on the way down. He was about 20, diabetic and running out of food. I gave him a candy bar which seemed to help his situation. He still had a few options in his bear canister and was trying to finish quickly before all his food was gone. Although he wanted me to climb Forester Pass with him, I was shot and stopped mid-afternoon about two miles short of the pass. I was shooting for a big hike in the morning to get near Whitney in one more day.

The spot I stopped looked like the last good camping option before the pass. There was a stream and several small tent sites among the few trees growing at 11,000 feet. Apparently I wasn't the only person thinking that way. Over the next few hours several folks I had previously met on the trail pulled into the area. Richard (Florida), Frick and Frack (brothers from Los Angeles), Mike (Illinois) and a group of four from Seattle all set up camp with the tentative plan to summit Mount Whitney in two days.

There were some pretty entertaining conversations that evening as we watched a storm hitting the higher elevations just above us. Luckily, we stayed dry. Richard and I decided to get an early start in the morning so we'd be over the 13,000-foot Forester Pass before any afternoon storms could build.

Where's Forester Pass?

Chapter 32: Pushing to New Heights

There was a dusting of snow above us, but camp was cold and dry when I awoke. I was a bit dizzy, but chalked the issue up to altitude. Richard and I were the first people moving, getting rolling about 7. It was a hard climb through rubble towards Forester, the highest pass of the entire trail. After 90 minutes or so, we met Shane and Melody enjoying breakfast among the rock piles. They had actually camped there. According to Shane, they had spent nearly an hour rearranging rocks to create a spot flat enough to pitch their tent. That made no sense to me. Spending that hour walking would have put them over the pass and close to a flat spot with water. Apparently it's hard to beat the comfort of an exposed semi-level bed of rocks. Maybe I'm missing out.

Richard at Shane and Melody's campsite

A half hour later I was standing at 13,180 feet, the crest of Forester Pass. There was a bit of smoke in the air, but the view was still outstanding. The drop off the pass was pretty dramatic with some serious switchbacks, so it seemed like a good time for a break. Three ladies that worked for the National Park Service were also there cooking up breakfast and were a wealth of information. I found out just how close I could get to Mt. Whitney before I'd need to poop in a bag and carry it with me. (I was still worried about the learning curve of using a "wag bag.")

Relaxing at Forester Pass

In addition, they confirmed a rumor for us. Apparently it's true that if a pack mule dies on the trail high up on a mountain, the corpse is dynamited. The thought process is: burial is impossible in the rocks, a large carcass would take forever to decompose in the dry alpine environment and eventually it would attract bears. Of course if a bear was squatting on a dead mule, that might close the trail for weeks at a time. By exploding the body, smaller predators can handle most of it and the rest can quickly decompose. I didn't ask about humans. Hopefully, I can finish the trail in one piece.

After the initial drop, the trail leveled out somewhat, but generally dropped for the next 10 miles. I walked most of the stretch alone, enjoying the sights. The area was obviously very dry and there were few trees to block the views, or the sun. It reminded me somewhat of desert hikes I've taken in Arizona. Near the High Sierra Trail I got into some trees and took a break for a late lunch. Richard, Frick and Frack caught up to me and we walked together for a while.

Frack pushing up the slope

Despite the long drop the trail was still bouncing around 11,000 feet. Between the altitude and being tired from earlier climbs each uphill was pretty tough. Eventually the trail swung east, the Pacific Crest Trail split off and we were looking at a heck of a big mountain in front of us. From the size of it, we could only assume we were looking at Mount Whitney and the finish of the JMT.

Looks like Whitney ahead

Though it was only mid-afternoon, I was getting pretty worn out. It appeared everyone else was just as tired as I was ahead of the rest of the group. Clouds were building up around Whitney and it looked like I'd be getting wet in the not too distant future. Once the lightning started, I picked up the pace hoping to make it to a camping area before the storm cut loose.

The trail and I stayed on the edge of the storm and dry for the next mile or so until I reached Crabtree Junction. There was tree cover, a pretty stream, plenty of places to camp and I was still dry. After covering 15 miles I was ready to stop. However, I was still 7 ½ tough miles from the top of Whitney and I felt I should get a little closer. To finish in a day I'd not only need to tackle that climb, but also walk another 10 ½ miles off the mountain to the trailhead at Whitney Portal. Once I sat down for a few minutes though, I knew it would be tough to go any further. It looked like the next day might need to be a long one.

Richard, Frick and Frack rolled in about 30 minutes later. I asked if they wanted to hike some more and get a little closer to Whitney. "Hell no!" was the consensus and they began setting up camp around me. It turned out to be a great place to camp. Some deer walked by as I filtered water. The storm stayed up on the mountain and never reached us. There was even a toilet in the area. Not a latrine mind you, but a toilet with a view.

Hope you weren't looking for privacy

After some heated discussion among themselves, Frick and Frack announced they were only going to hike to Guitar Lake in the morning. Generally that is where most people start the assault on Whitney. It's about 2 ½ miles from where we were and 1,000 foot higher in elevation. Richard had a plane to catch and was heading for the finish. For better or worse, the closer I get to finishing a hike, the more I tend to push myself. In addition, we were near the end of hiking season and a big snow could hit the higher elevations at any time. Richard and I planned to get up around 4 am and make a run for it.

The rain that threatened Crabtree Junction all evening long never reached where we were camping. I got up at 4 am and the sky was ablaze with stars. The display rivaled any I'd seen. The Milky Way was obvious and I'm sure I would've spotted a few satellites had I taken the time. I was on a mission however. After a quick breakfast of the last of my peanut butter and tortillas I packed up my tent for, hopefully, the last time on this trip.

Richard was also soon ready to roll. His breakfast was a combination of instant Starbucks coffee, Carnation Instant Breakfast and powdered milk mixed into some cold water. It looked and sounded pretty rough but it was how he started every morning. After an initial slug of the concoction he was ready to roll. Headlamps pushed back the darkness as we started the long climb towards Mt Whitney.

The trail was pretty obvious and the glow of the headlamps was enough to navigate without much trouble. On the 2 ½ miles to Guitar Lake the elevation rose 800 feet to 11,500. The steady climb was enough to keep me warm despite rather cool temperatures. Before I got there though, I told Richard I was going to step off the trail for a few minutes. He readily agreed and said he'd be doing the same. We were running out of time to legally "shit in the woods" and neither of us wanted to be stuck on Whitney, using the "wag bags" we'd been carrying the entire trip.

The sky was just starting to lighten in the east when we made it to Guitar Lake. A number of hikers had obviously camped there the night before and several headlamps could be seen moving upward in the distance. A small, partially frozen stream was running into the lake and we stopped there to filter enough water for the climb. Per my guide, that would be the last opportunity until a good distance past the summit. Richard loaded up with three liters and I carried two. Like with food, I prioritized light weight over adequate supply. We left the area a bit after 6 am with a five mile and 3,000-foot climb to the peak.

Guitar Lake at dawn

The trail was pretty consistent above Guitar Lake, using switchbacks to climb around 600 feet per mile. However, each step higher also meant a bit less oxygen. At the top there is less than 60% of the oxygen found at sea level. Combined with the cold, once I passed 12,000 feet, I really started feeling it.

The trail surface was pretty good, so that was a plus. It was important to be a bit careful around any wet area as it was frozen. There were a few other hikers in the area. Whenever I met one, I always stopped and chatted. If nothing else, each break allowed me to catch my breath somewhat.

Richard grinding up the trail

The day remained clear and, at that altitude, the sun was strong. Things were quickly warming up. By 8:30 I had made it to the Mount Whitney Trail. The intersection was about two miles and 1,000 feet from the summit. Many hikers drop their packs at this point as they can be picked back up on the way down and there were several laying by the trail. There were also several marmots hanging around waiting for an opportunity to check the packs for food.

Nice looking pack you have there.

I stuck a small bag of trail mix in my pocket. I made sure what little other food I had left was in the bear canister, pulled the canister out of the pack and left the pack open. Grabbing a half liter of water, I started for the top.

Free from the pack, the next half mile felt great, but soon the lack of oxygen began weighing me down again. In addition, the trail got a bit "sketchy" as it climbed through boulder fields and along steep drops. I was walking slower and slower as I went. The last quarter mile was a fairly gentle climb, but even that was difficult. Finally, I made the summit at 10 am. I was at 14,505 feet, the highest spot in the continental United States and the completion point of the John Muir Trail! Now all I had to do was get off the mountain via a ten-mile trail that dropped nearly 7,000 feet. Oh, and find a way 13 more miles to the town of Lone Pine. That could wait though. I was taking a few minutes to enjoy the view and my completion of the trail.

View from the top

There were several hikers on the summit including Evan, who I had hiked with earlier. I was glad to see he had made it despite his shortage of food and diabetes. At that point, he was completely out of food. I told him if we met up once I was back to my pack, he could have any food I had left. Shane and Melody were also there. Richard made the summit about 20 minutes behind me. Eventually though, since I was no longer climbing, I began to get cold. It was time to start down. I did try to call the Dow Villa in Lone Pine. It was a hotel recommended to me, but I couldn't get a signal. Oh well.

Heading down took considerably less effort and I was soon back at my pack. It appeared undisturbed. Richard's pack was covered with dusty marmot footprints, but I didn't notice any damage. Evan showed up right behind me and I gave him an energy bar and a couple instant oatmeal packets. I'd never seen anyone eat oatmeal dry before, but I guess if you need the glucose, you do what you have to do. Somebody else was there with a box of cookies and we both got a fistful of those. It looked like Evan was set for a while.

Shane and Melody also showed up at that point. Melody was in bad shape as her one boot had completely fallen apart. Her feet were a mess and she was looking at walking the next 10 miles in just socks. I had a small roll of duct tape with me and offered it to her. She used the whole roll rebuilding her boot, but it looked like it might hold her for the rest of the day. As a way of thanking me, she mentioned that she and Shane had a car at the trailhead and, if we finished together, I had a ride into town.

With that, they took off at a fast clip, bouncing through the first of 100 downhill switchbacks like pinballs. I looked at Evan and we both yanked on our packs and gave chase.

One of the 100 switchbacks

The downhill was unrelenting and the pounding took its toll. I was tired but there was no way I was going to miss that ride. The stretch was as steep as any on the trail, and went on for 8 ½ miles. While the downhill was tough, doing that section uphill would have been much more difficult. Hiking the JMT south to north would be a herculean effort. I couldn't imagine starting my hike by carrying a week's worth of food up that climb.

The scenery stayed beautiful the whole way, though I rarely stopped for pictures. Evan and I stuck together and discussed life, including his struggles with Juvenile Diabetes. That he was able to finish his hike was amazing. While the hike seemed endless at the time, we did cover the mileage pretty quick. Less than four hours from leaving the summit of Whitney, we were at Melody's car. She took off her boots and started to cry. I looked at her feet and almost got sick. That was one tough young woman. Before we got rolling, I was able to get through to the Dow Villa and rent their last room for the night.

Melody drove like she hiked so we were in town in no time. First stop was McDonalds for some well-deserved empty calories. From there, Shane and Melody were heading home to Bakersfield and I was heading across the street to the Dow Villa. Evan needed to make arrangements to meet his parents and gave his Mom a call. It was pretty interesting to hear him excitedly tell his Mom about his hike. It was also gratifying to hear him tell her that a guy named Jim happened along when he was having trouble, gave him some food and "saved the hike."

The Dow Villa was a great place with a great shower. Of course it was the first shower I'd had in eight days so that may have affected my opinion. Richard called a bit later. Apparently "some bastard" had got the last room at the Dow Villa and he was bunking down the street at the local hostel. I bought him a beer at the Pizza Factory to make up for his bad luck.

In the morning it was a $19 bus ride (a cab would have been $550) back near the entrance of Yosemite. Rather than wait a day for bus service into the park, 10 minutes of hitchhiking got me back to my truck. Beyond that, a three-day drive and I was home from a tremendous adventure.

Chapter 33: The Trails are Waiting

"Of all the paths you take in life, make sure a few of them are dirt."

John Muir

There's scenery, wildlife, comradery, and adventure on all long trails, but they are not the only rewards for the effort. Though it doesn't always seem that way at the time, challenging conditions add to the satisfaction and make the effort worthwhile. Certainly, you can drive nearly to the top of Mount Mansfield on the Long Trail. You hardly have to hike at all to get to the summit. The view might be the same for all, but the experience is not. The challenge improves the experience in a way that can't be measured; only felt. As Mark Obmascik stated in his book <u>Halfway to Heaven: My White-knuckled—and Knuckleheaded—Quest for the Rocky Mountain High</u>, *"I'll fly on a plane and people will look out the window at thirty thousand feet and say, 'Isn't this view good enough for you?' And I say no, it's not good enough. I didn't earn it. In the mountains, I earn it."*

Beyond the pride, satisfaction and beautiful views found at the completion of a big climb, there are other rewards from a long hike. Conversations with fellow hikers, sharing the trail with other animals at the top of the food chain, the picturesque waterfall, the elk in the distance, the rustle of leaves in the dark and the first bit of sun after a storm are all compensation for the "work" of the long hike. For me, it runs even deeper. For 10,000 generations or more, humans were hunters and gatherers; a nomadic people immersed in nature. Our very DNA has been honed to not only survive but thrive while wandering in the woods. To live that way, if even just for a short time on a trail, isn't just good for the mind and body; it's good for the soul.

So there it is, my experience as a thru-hiker. Yours could be even better. Think of the stories you'll have. Each of these trails is long enough to be an epic adventure, but short enough to be achievable.

Not to sound too dark, but you're not getting any younger. None of us are. Remember, no one ever laid on their deathbed wishing they had spent more time watching TV, playing video games or surfing the Internet for cat videos. A life changing experience is attainable. There's no better time than now to start planning your grand adventure, whatever it may be. The trails are waiting. The mountains are waiting. Your soul is waiting.

Chapter 34: The Gear Lowdown

While I don't proclaim to be a backpacking gear expert, I did spend quite a bit of time researching, testing and living with the gear I used on the trail. It may have been just luck, but all my equipment worked, for the most part, flawlessly. The majority of the gear listed below was used on all three trails. That's a total of about 1,000 miles in pretty varied conditions. Not counting food, water and the bear canister, my pack weight ran around 20 pounds.

Pack – Osprey Exos 58, size large. The pack weighs only 2 lb, 12 ounce and has a 61 liter volume. It was comfortable handling a 25-30 pound load, but carried close to 40 lb. when necessary.

Tent – Big Agnes Copper Spur UL 1 which only tips the scale at 2 lb, 3 ounce, is self-standing and was big enough that, at 6 foot, 3 inches, I didn't feel overly cramped. It set up quick and at times held up to some significant storms. Ventilation could have been better, but it wasn't bad. For another 4.5 ounces I got the footprint as well.

Sleeping Bag – I used two bags. In August on the Long Trail, I brought a Sea To Summit Traveller Tr1. The EN temperature rating was 50 degrees and the long version weighed 17 ounces. When combined with a silk liner (4.5 ounce), I could sleep comfortably to the mid-40s. At other times I carried the Sierra Designs Zissou 23. The bag weighed 2 lb, 3 ounce in long. The EN comfort rating is 34 degrees for women and 23 for men. The bags used either water resistant "Dri-Down" or "Ultra-Dry Down" in their construction. I never "wet the bag" to test the capability, though they both stayed warm when damp from wet weather or condensation.

Pad – I used another pad on the CT, but switched to the Exped Hyperlite. I used the medium version that weighs 12 ounces. Despite the light weight, the pad has a 3.3 R-value and a seemingly tough outer skin.

Cooking kit - GSI Outdoors Pinnacle Soloist Cookset. The pot, lid, cup and a foldable spoon weigh in at just under 10 ounces (leave the storage sack at home). My no name, folding canister stove fits inside the pot, and weighs 4 ounces. My stove cost less than ten bucks yet nothing, including the built-in igniter, ever failed. Google "cheap camping stove" and it should be at the top of the list. A small gas canister also fits in the pot, weighs 8 ounces full, and lasted five days or more when heating water for instant oatmeal in the morning and a wholesome freeze-dried dinner at night.

Water Filter/Storage – Sawyer Mini Filter with a one liter squeeze bag. I also used a small "bottled water" bottle to dip in the creeks to fill the squeeze bottle. Filtered water was kept in a one liter Nalgene bottle (the soft ones are lighter) and a one liter Gatorade bottle (lighter still). I also brought some chlorine dioxide tablets for back up. Everything together, except the actual water, weighed in at 12 ounces.

Small "essentials" – Petzl Tikka Plus headlamp weighed 4 oz including the lithium batteries that lasted weeks at a time. Small folding knife at 2 oz. Twenty five feet of rope to hang food at 3 oz. Pack rain cover at 4 oz. Small first aid kit at 4 oz which included a few Band-Aids, a gauze pad, tape, alcohol pads, anti-bacterial pads, sting relief pad, blister covers and a small anti-friction stick.

Smaller "essentials" – compass, mini camera tripod, small roll of duct tape, small container of insect repellent, 2 lighters, bug head net (never used), small multi-tool, small pepper spray (to irritate bears…never used), sleeping pad repair kit (never used), sewing needle (never used) and Neo-Air inflatable seat. Everything together weighed 8-10 oz.

Guides for various trails that weighed 4-6 oz.

Toiletries – Toilet paper, sanitizer, contact lens solution, case and mirror, toothbrush and paste, Aleve, aspirin, Advil PM, Imodium (never used), Wet Ones hand/face wipes and sunscreen. Total weight of 14 oz.

Clothing – Typically I was wearing either North Face or REI nylon zip off pants/shorts, Smartwool lightweight t-shirt, short REI socks, nylon ball cap and Exofficio underwear. Spares in the pack were one pair of underwear, two pair of socks, light nylon pants, a 100 weight Columbia fleece pullover, Under Armor t-shirt, cheap rain pants, Outdoor Research packable rain jacket and in colder conditions, an REI down vest, nylon gloves and watchman's cap. Crammed in Ziploc bags, the extra clothes weighed 3-3½ lbs. I never suffered from a lack of clothes, but at one time or another I did use every item of extra clothing.

Shoes - I started out fairly lightweight with Saucony Xodus trail runners. The size 13 pair tipped the scales just over 2 lbs. Later, the Merrill Capra hiking shoes weighed about 6 ounces more. In the pack was a 1lb, 1 oz pair of "camp" sandals.

Electronics –The Spot Satellite Messenger weighed 5oz. I used it on a daily basis to let friend(s) and family know where I was and that I was OK. Luckily I never had to try the buttons that told them I was lost, had a shattered pelvis or lost a fight with a moose.

My iPhone with a waterproof case weighed 8 oz, and was used as a backup camera, GPS, Kindle book reader, journal, and as a phone with texts, email and internet when I had cell service.

My dedicated camera was a Canon SX 160 that weighed 10 oz. While it took some great shots, the pictures from the iPhone look, in many instances, as good or better.

There are ways to lower this weight, and many easy ways to increase it, but other than always needing to carry more food, I felt like I had everything necessary to stay comfortable on the trail under normal circumstances.